MARIJUANA GARDEN SAVER

NUTRIENT IMBALANCES

Calcium Deficiency

Iron Deficiency

Magnesium Deficiency

Nitrogen Deficiency

Phosphorous Deficiency

Potassium Deficiency

Zinc Deficiency

Boron Deficiency

Also includes pH problems, copper, manganese, molybdeunum, silicon, and sulfur deficiencies

PEST INVASIONS

Ants

Aphids

Corn Borers

Fungus Gnats

Mealybugs

Broad Mites

Russet Mites

Thrips

Also includes information on spider mites, caterpillars, deer, leaf miners, moles and rats.

PLANT DISEASES

Algae

Gray Mold

Leaf Septoria

Powdery mildew

Fusarium

Pythium

Brown Mold

Wilt

ENVIRONMENTAL STRESSES

Airy, loose buds

Clones

Fluorescent burn

Hermaphrodites

Nutrient burn

Stretching

High temperature

When to water

Marijuana Garden Saver: A Field Guide to Identifying and Diagnosing Cannabis Problems

Copyright © 2019 Ed Rosenthal Published by Quick American
A Division of Quick Trading Co. Piedmont, CA, USA

ISBN: 978-1-93680743-7 eISBN: 978-1-936807-44-4

Printed in the United States Fourth Printing

Editor and Project Director: Rolph Blythe
Contributing Editors: Laurie Casebier, Matthew Gates, Joshua Sheets,
Darcy Thompson, Greg Zeman
Art Director: Christian Petke
Design: Scott Idleman/Blink
Cover Design: Scott Idleman, Christian Petke
Cover Photography: Ed Rosenthal
Back cover photo by Lizzy Fritz of Farmhands

Library of Congress Control Number: 2019937100

The material offered in this book is presented as information that should be available
to the public. The Publisher does not advocate breaking the law. We urge readers to
support secure passage of fair marijuana legislation.

MARIJUANA GARDEN SAVER

A Field Guide to Identifying and Correcting Cannabis Problems

By Ed Rosenthal

Dedicated to Sister Mary Etienne Tibeau, a fine researcher.

ACKNOWLEDGEMENTS
Kristen Angelo (A Pot Farmers Daughter), Rolph Blythe, Arya Campbell, Julia Hass, Scott Idleman, Jane Klein, Fred Morlege, Christian Petke, James Rushing, Marisa Sympson, Darcy Thompson

Nothing is for certain, it could always go wrong.
Come in when it's rainin; go out when it's gone.

We could have us a high time, living the
good life.

High Time
The Grateful Dead
Lyricist: Robert Hunter

CONTENTS

INTRODUCTION
HOW TO USE THIS BOOK

Marijuana Garden Saver gives you the tools you need to grow healthy marijuana plants. This book is a troubleshooting guide for people who are growing cannabis. It is meant to take you over the bumps and help you solve garden problems. Using the information provided here, you will be able to navigate garden problems and reach harvest with abundant high-quality bud from your garden.

Section 1 provides information about proper nutrients the plants need and how to identify deficiencies, and includes a guide to pH management.

Section 2 covers pests that are most attracted to cannabis, their effect on the plant and a variety of preventive and problem-solving techniques.

Section 3 identifies common diseases that can attack marijuana and how they may be prevented and controlled.

Section 4 reviews environmental stresses that can impact a garden.

Section 5 is a guide to the controls referenced in the preceding sections, with suggested commercial brands.

Photo by Fred Morledge

Photo by David Downs, taken at SPARC

Section 1

NUTRIENTS

When plants cannot get the nutrients they need they do not function properly, adversely affecting growth and yield. This can occur in any growing medium, while using any planting mix or technique—coir, rock wool, soil, soilless, hydroponic or aeroponic. Plant disorders are characterized by their symptoms which appear more quickly in hydroponic gardens than in planting mixes or soil.

An over-abundance of nutrients can result in nutrient burn or toxicity and can also lock out other ingredients. Unless the damage is slight, individual leaves do not recover from nutrient deficiencies. Some nutrients are mobile and are translocated from older to new growth so the damage is seen in older leaves, not in new growth. Other nutrients are not mobile. Their deficiencies are apparent in the new growth.

All fertilizer packages list three numbers that identify the N-P-K ratio. They usually appear as three numbers with dashes between them such as 25-10-10. The first number represents Nitrogen (N), which is responsible for foliage or leaf development. Fertilizers that promote heavy leaf growth have a higher first number (N) than the other two. The second number represents Phosphorus (P), which is important for strong stems and flowering. The third number is Potassium (K), which promotes healthy metabolic function. Sometimes micronutrients are listed after the macronutrients: these are Calcium (Ca), Copper (Cu), Manganese (Mn), and Zinc (Zn).

All nutrients are required to be present for proper metabolic function. Most growers use premixed nutrient systems and faithfully follow the manufacturer's feed schedules never see deficiencies before they flush their plants. Two deficiencies that may appear when using commercial fertilizers are Calcium (Ca) and Magnesium (Mg). On the other hand, organic, living soil and outdoor plants that do not receive supplemental nutrition are more often subject to deficiencies, but only because living soil systems have more variables involved in delivering nutrients compared to concentrated nutrient products.

pH

pH is a logarithmic measure of the acid-alkaline balance in soil or water. A pH of 1 is the most acidic solution, 7 is neutral and 14 is the most alkaline. When the pH is within the 5.8-6.3 range, slightly acid, the nutrients dissolve well and are available to the plants. As the pH rises above or falls below those numbers some nutrients precipitate out of solution. Plants cannot absorb nutrients when they are precipitated. Plants can only "drink" them when they are in solution so even if nutrients are present, they are only available to the plants only when they are dissolved. As a result, even though sufficient nutrients may be present, plant roots do not have access to them so and the plants will indicate deficiencies. Plants that are growing in water or soil outside the proper pH range grow very slowly.

Different species of plants have adapted to living under different pH levels. Marijuana has been grown in hydroponic solutions with a pH as low as 5.5, but it does best when grown in soil or water within a pH range of 5.6-6.3, slightly acidic. This is the pH of good garden soils. All plant nutrients are water soluble in this range so they are readily available to the plants. Outside this range some become less available.

pH can be viewed as a see-saw. As fertilizers are added it can drop or rise rapidly. It's up to the grower to keep it the pH stable. It is important to measure pH after adding nutrients. When pH levels are out of the "safe" range nutrients fall out of solution and are unavailable to the plants. pH is important for both soil and hydroponic gardening. Failing to monitor it can lead to disastrous results. The pH level directly affects plants' ability to absorb nutrients. When the pH rises above 6.2 some micronutrients precipitate out of solution and are less available. Below 5.5 Boron (B), Copper (Cu), Manganese (Mn), and Phosphorous (P) become too available. This can result in toxicity.

The only accurate way to adjust the pH is by using a pH meter or pH test papers. Guesswork won't do.

ADJUSTING YOUR PH OUTDOORS & IN

Outdoors, if you are adjusting the soil pH before planting, use powdered sulfur if the soil is too alkaline or lime if it is too acidic. Check with knowledgeable local nursery staff or agricultural extension agents familiar with local soils. They can give you advice on correct proportions since soils vary in their reaction to adjustments. It takes several months after the addition of these minerals for the soil to adjust.

If the plants are already in the ground and the soil is out of the preferred range, adjust the irrigation water using pH up to raise alkalinity or pH down to increase acidity. Monitor the runoff. For instance, a composed media had a

Made from all natural ingredients, TNB Up / TNB Down will raise and lower pH levels of hydroponic or liquid fertilizer systems; this makes for healthy plants and lush gardens.

pH of over 8, which is very alkaline. It was irrigated with water adjusted to a pH of 5.1, very acidic. At first the runoff was over 7. Eventually the runoff tested at 6 and the pH level of the irrigation water was adjusted higher to maintain that pH in the runoff.

Water should be pH adjusted only after soluble fertilizers are added to it because their ingredients also affect water pH.

Most commercial potting soils and topsoil are already pH balanced. If the plants are to be grown in soil or planting mix, check the pH using a pH meter or test strips before you plant.

Most indoor planting media are not soils at all: they are made using bark, peat moss or coir as the main ingredient. Other materials are added to adjust porosity and water retention. These mixes can be considered disease-and pest-free.

Planting mixes can be adjusted using commercially available pH-up and pH-down mixtures. Home remedies are available but can cause problems. Commercial products tend to be more stable and are concentrated and inexpensive.

IMMOBILE VS. MOBILE NUTRIENTS

One way to diagnose nutrient problems is by their location. Some nutrients are immobile. Once they are set in place in the plant, they cannot move from their location. Other nutrients are mobile. When there is a limited supply, they go where the action is—usually to the top of the canopy.

IMMOBILE MINERALS

Boron (B), Calcium (Ca), Copper (Cu), Iron (Fe), Manganese (Mn), Molybdenum (Mb), Sulfur (S) and Zinc (Zn) are utilized by the plant in ways that prevent them from being moved or movable on a limited scale. These are called immobile or intermediately movable nutrients. Calcium, for example, is permanently laid down in cell walls and cannot be moved. When these nutrients are deficient, the plant cannot transport them from older leaves so new growth occurs where immobile nutrient deficiency symptoms show up as deformed leaves. With extreme deficiency they may die back. This is most likely to happen with Boron and Calcium deficiencies.

MOBILE NUTRIENTS

Nutrients that the plant can move around are called mobile nutrients. Nitrogen (N), Magnesium (Mg), Phosphorous (P), Potassium (K), and Nickel (Ni) are examples. These nutrients can be cannibalized and moved to support new growth elsewhere in the plant.

When there is a deficiency, plants typically move the nutrients from old growth to the top of the canopy, where they will be utilized most effectively. Deficiency symptoms then show up on the older leaves from which the nutrients are being removed.

Nutrient deficiencies can, at times, serve a purpose—for both the plant and the grower. If you have grown cannabis before and flushed your plants at the end of flowering, you are already familiar with nutrient deficiencies. Flushing

A yellowed leaf in the lower canopy is an indicator that nutrients are moving elsewhere in the plant.

removes nutrients from the root zone, cutting the plant off from getting the materials it needs to grow. Without an incoming supply of nutrients, plants (including cannabis) can adapt to periods of low nutrients and move some nutrients around via the xylem and phloem of the vascular system to support new growth.

Flushing starves the plant of all nutrients, creating multiple simultaneous deficiencies. Both fertilized and non-supplemented grows sometimes experience a single deficiency. In these cases, the appearance of symptoms among older generations of leaves while new growth remains healthy matches expectations for one or more deficiencies among the mobile nutrients. Deficiency symptoms of immobile nutrients show up in new growth while older leaves remain healthy looking.

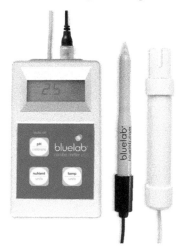

Bluelab's Combo Meter Plus ensures your nutrient solution is at the right level and available to your plants. This 3 in 1 device will measure your pH levels, nutrient levels & temperatures directly in your solution, to optimize nutrient availability through the growing system.

INVEST IN A GOOD SET OF PH AND EC/TDS METERS

Invest in two relatively inexpensive meters: a pH meter and a TDS meter. The pH meter tells whether the soil chemistry is right for good uptake, and the TDS meter quickly tells growers whether there are too little, enough or too many nutrients in the root zone. Total dissolved solids (TDS) are measured in parts per million (ppm).

A low TDS suggests a general lack of nutrients. Check the actual readings against the projected numbers printed on the instruction label. Then adjust the strength of the nutrient solution or frequency of delivery.

The TDS meter won't highlight which nutrients are lacking, just the total amount in solution. The only way to measure the individual nutrient levels on-site is by using chemical test kits. Micronutrients are present in such small amounts compared to the major nutrients that all of the minors could be left out of a nutrient batch and the TDS value would still be 98-99% of the target value.

The only way to accurately determine deficiencies is by recognizing them or by submitting soil or nutrient solution samples to a lab.

pH and TDS meters are available for solutions as well. To measure pH and TDS in the root zone the grower has to add enough distilled water to the container to get a small amount of runoff liquid out of the bottom of the container. These meters can then measure pH and TDS of that sample.

This is a painful, time-consuming and highly variable process. To measure levels in mediums, use a meter whose probes are inserted into media for quick and direct measurements.

Don't forget the roots when you are checking for symptoms. The roots should be white and firm. Brown, blackened, mushy or stringy roots indicate symptoms of problems.

In hydroponic systems, monitor the nutrient/water solution a minimum of once a week. If the numbers haven't changed much and the plants are growing rapidly, there is usually no reason to change nutrients. If the nutrients need to be changed, rinse the roots at the same time. This helps prevent bacterial or fungal growth that attacks cannabis roots.

A really low EC (electrical conductivity) suggests a general lack of nutrients. Supplemental growers can then adjust the strength of their nutrient solutions or frequency of nutrient delivery. Unfortunately, the EC won't tell you if minor nutrients are deficient because, unlike major nutrients, they are present in such small amounts that they could be left out of a nutrient batch and the EC would still be 98-99% of the target value. Aside from visually recognizing deficiency and toxicity symptoms, the only way to absolutely identify a deficiency is by submitting soil and nutrient solution samples to a lab.

DIAGNOSING NUTRIENT DEFICIENCIES

Nutrient deficiencies appear without uniformity across a plant's leaves early in a deficiency scenario. The symptoms are apparent on either newer growth or older growth so if there is uniformity in symptoms throughout the plant, the problem is not likely to be a deficiency.

If the symptoms are visible only on newer or only on older growth, a nutrient deficiency is highly probable.

Once a nutrient problem is confirmed, you need to know how to solve it. Be aware, many of the visual symptoms presented as nutrient deficiencies and toxicities can also be created by disease and environmental factors, which are discussed in subsequent chapters in this book.

Visual Diagnostic Key of Nutrient Deficiencies

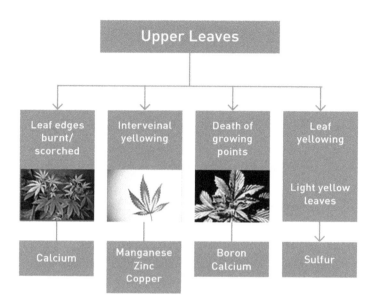

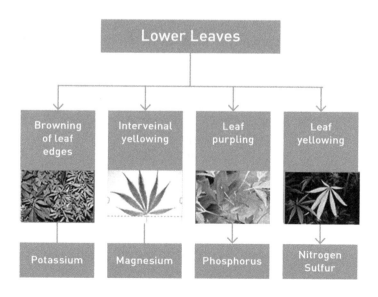

DEFICIENCY SAMPLES

Look at the growing points of stems and branches to detect potential nutrient issues.

If older generations of leaves display mottling, yellowing between veins, or drying or dying of mature leaves, the symptoms match those of deficiencies of the mobile nutrients N, P, K or Mg (Nitrogen, Phosphorus, Potassium or Magnesium). Plants scavenge these nutrients from older leaves. New growth appears healthy while the symptoms appear in the cannibalized leaves.

If new growth appears stunted, deformed, brown or dying, think deficiency of an immobile nutrient. B, Ca, Cu, Fe, Mn, Mb, S and Zn (Boron, Calcium, Copper, Iron, Manganese, Molybdenum, Sulfur and Zinc are immobile so the plant cannot move them and symptoms appear on new growth).

Yellowing of new-growth leaves matches the description of iron deficiency. Sulfur deficiency, while much rarer, also results in these symptoms.

Purpling of stems may be characteristic of certain strains, a sign of a phosphorus deficiency or normal plant response to cool temperatures.

Patterns of chlorosis (yellowing) in leaves suggests deficiencies of both major and minor elements.

For all deficiency symptoms:

- Review nutrient recipe and mixing protocols to ensure that all the nutrients required are being delivered. For users of commercial concentrated nutrients, this means making sure the manufacturer's recommendations are followed. Even so, there may be Ca and Mg deficiencies if runoff, rainwater or R/O water is used. For DIY nutrient mixers be sure the recipe is complete (all nutrients) and delivering the proper levels.
- Review the pH of nutrient solutions and media if possible to make sure the pH does not drop below 5.6.
- Plants can be and are being grown successfully outdoors in soils with a pH as low as 5 or as high as 8 and still allow for adequate uptake of all nutrients even if it may not be optimal. Growth would be enhanced by lowering pH so more nutrients dissolved. Plants can be grown outdoors in soil with a pH as low as 5 or as high as 8. Yields will suffer, however.

DIAGNOSING NUTRIENT TOXICITIES

Excessive nutrient levels often result in nutrients bonding with other nutrients to create goopy solids that fall out of solution making them unavailable for plants to uptake. This can produce any number of other deficiencies with hard to predict visual symptoms.

If leaves appear to be significantly darker green and are smaller than usual, think high nitrogen, possibly due to a general over fertilization. Dark green is not normal for cannabis.

If leaves are dark and hooked downward resembling a claw, think excess nitrogen. Pests can cause hooking too no matter what the color so be sure to check for thrips in particular. If you don't see pests but the leaves are dark, it is likely excess nitrogen.

If plants are growing poorly, check the roots. If they are blackened and stringy this is a symptom of highly excessive nutrient delivery. If you find burnt roots, remove and destroy all affected plants.

Photo by Kristen Angelo

TOXICITY SYMPTOMS

For all toxicity symptoms:

- Flush with water for two days. Follow this procedure for container and "in the ground" growing.
- Review/correct nutrient recipes to ensure proper levels of nutrients and no mixing problems.
- Reintroduce fertilization after two days and monitor plant response.

Nitrogen deficiency

IDENTIFYING SPECIFIC NUTRIENT DEFICIENCIES AND TOXICITIES

This section includes illustrations that represent the symptoms plants get when they have deficiencies. Use these pictures and descriptions to help you think through a diagnosis and use meters or labs to provide data that can help confirm visual symptoms.

To make the section easy to navigate, we begin each description with a quick reality check about the problem: How common is it?

This is followed by a description of the affected plant's appearance. Next is information on the role that the nutrient plays in the plant's nutrition and its mobility. By mobility we mean that once a nutrient is transported to a site and is used to build tissue, can it be moved or is it fixed? Mobile nutrients move to new growth so deficiencies appear on older vegetation. Nonmobile nutrients stay put so that deficiencies appear on new growth. Each nutrient section concludes with a guide to fixing the deficiency and getting the plant back to full health.

DEFICIENCIES OF NUTRIENT ELEMENTS IN CANNABIS

Suspected element—

Symptoms	N	P	K	Mg	Fe	Cu	Zn	B	Mo	Mn	Over-fertilization
Yellowing of:											
Younger leaves					x					x	
Middle leaves									x		
Older leaves	x		x	x			x				
Between veins					x					x	
Old leaves drop	x										
Leaf curl over				x							
Leaf curl under			x			x					x
Leaf tips burn:											
Younger leaves								x			
Older leaves	x						x				
Young leaves wrinkle & curl			x				x	x	x		
Necrosis			x	x	x		x			x	
Leaf growth stunted	x	x									
Dark green/purplish leaves and stems		x									
Pale green leaf color	x								x		
Mottling							x				
Spindly	x										
Soft stems	x		x								
Hard/brittle stems		x	x								
Growing tips die			x					x			
Stunted root growth		x									
Wilting						x					

Boron deficiency

BORON (B)

How common is it?

Boron (B) deficiency is rare. It occurs very occasionally in some western and sandy soils. In planting mixes it can be washed out by overwatering. B is very soluble at pH levels to 6. As the pH rises it becomes less soluble and is mostly precipitated at pH 7.

Symptoms

The first sign of a B deficiency is the browning or graying of the growing tips followed by their death. Soon after, the lateral shoots start to grow but then die. Shoots appear sunburned, twisted and in a bright green color. The leaves develop small, brown necrotic dead spots that look like strawberry seeds and are surrounded by an area of dying tissue between leaf veins. B deficiency resembles a Ca deficiency but can be differentiated by the small size of the necrotic areas.

Stems and petioles (leaf stems) are brittle and show signs of hollowness.

Roots become stunted and the smaller secondary roots become short and swollen as the root tips die. The roots are vulnerable to fungal and bacterial attacks that rot the root hairs and cause discoloration.

Mobility
B is immobile. Its deficiency affects only newer growth.

Toxicity
B toxicity is rare and is caused primarily by over fertilization. Its symptoms, which appear on new growth, are the yellowing of the leaf tips which progresses inward. The leaves drop and the plant dies.

An overabundance of free Ca sometimes prevents B absorption.

Role in plant nutrition
B is important in the processes of maturation, pollen germination and seed production. It also aids in cell division, protein formation, healthy leaf color and plant structure formation. Proper amounts keep stems, stalks and branches strong and help plant cells maintain rigidity. B helps Ca remain soluble.

Problem Solving
Treat a B deficiency foliarly (by spraying) or through the irrigation water, using 1 teaspoon of Borax (11% B) per 25 gallons water, 0.75 ounce per 100 gallons.

Solubor (20% B) is an agricultural product. Use 1 Teaspoon per 50 gallons, 0.4 ounce per 100 gallons. Both formulas supply 6 ppm B. Be careful in treating a deficiency. It's easy to use too much B, which will cause toxicity.

Calcium deficiency Photo by Mel Frank

CALCIUM (Ca)

How common is it?

Calcium (C) deficiency is rare outdoors except in sandy and very acidic soils. The deficiency is occasionally found in planting mixes and is more common in hydroponics. Ca deficiency sometimes occurs in soilless growing mediums that have not been supplemented with lime, which is composed mostly of calcium.

Rainwater, river runoff, distilled water and reverse osmosis water, as well as some tap water, lack significant amounts of dissolved Ca. This often leads to Ca deficiency unless the water is supplemented. Some fertilizers are too low in Ca to create an adequate supply.

Symptoms

Ca is semi-mobile so symptoms show up first in newer growth that fails to properly form and turns brown. Young shoots crinkle and turn yellow or purple. In severe cases they twist before they die. Large necrotic (dead) blotches of tan, dried tissue appear mostly on new growth but also on other plant parts along leaf edges. Necrosis appears along the lateral leaf margins. Problems migrate to the older growth, which browns and dies.

Stems and branches are weak, lack flexibility and crack easily.

The root system does not develop properly, leading to bacterial problems that cause root disease and die-off. The roots discolor to a sickly brown.

Mobility

Calcium is semi-mobile.

Role in plant nutrition

Ca strengthens plant cell walls and therefore stems, stalks and branches, and it aids in root growth—mostly the newer root hairs. It travels slowly and tends to concentrate in roots and older growth. Ca also enhances the uptake of K.

Kelp products contain a wide array of essential plant nutrients, vitamins and amino acids. Regular applications of Age Old® Kelp will provide plants with a myriad of beneficial substances that aid in overall plant growth and development, as well as increased microbial activity in the root zone. Age Old® Kelp is formulated with the purest Ascophyllum nodosum Sea Kelp harvested from the North Atlantic Ocean.

Photo: Turkish

Problem Solving

Both planting mediums and hydro systems can be fertilized as directed using a commercial liquid Ca-Mg formula; this provides instant availability to the plant. It can also be used in planting mixes. Commercial cannabis nutrient feed schedules deliver about 200 ppm of calcium. Most of the dissolved solids in municipal water are calcium so when municipal water is tested with a TDS/ppm meter and the result is 125 or less ppm, supplemental calcium will likely be necessary.

Calcium nitrate (CaNO3) is a water-soluble fertilizer that supplies both Ca and N. It is soluble and can also be used as a foliar spray. This formula gets Ca to the plant very quickly. Be careful not to add calcium nitrate during the flowering stage because it provides unwanted excess N.

Outdoors

Hydrated lime (also called liquid lime) can be added to soil and planting mixes. It is very fast-acting.

Dolomitic lime, which contains Mg as well as Ca, takes longer to absorb and is a good ingredient in planting mixes to prevent deficiency.

Garden lime can be added to planting mixes before potting. It provides calcium and also helps stabilize pH over time.

Add Ca to acidic soils to bring them into the pH range of 5.6-6.3. Use dolomitic lime or garden lime. Ground eggshells, fish bones and seashells also break down over the season and add calcium to the soil.

In hydroponic gardens a calcium/magnesium supplement is generally recommended. Every nutrient company manufactures one. Just check the label for concentration and dosage per gallon or liter. Take into account any additional nutrients present. If you're already high on N, use an additive without N in it.

General Discussion

Most planting mediums have adequate amounts of Ca. However, Ca should be added to the planting mix if the pH is too low. See the pH section for more information.

Hydroponically grown plants are most likely to suffer Ca deficiency.

Some hydro fertilizers contain only small amounts of Ca. The reason: some water systems have adequate mounts so no supplementation is needed. Since the amount of Ca dissolved in the supply water varies, hydro fertilizers supply a minimum amount. If the water supply contains more than 125 ppm of dissolved solids, it is probably providing the plants with enough Ca. If the water contains less than 100 ppm of dissolved solids, Ca-Mg should be added to the water. To find out how hard or soft your water is, you will need to have a TDS/ppm meter or refer to the local water district quality report. If the meter reads 125 ppm or more, no supplementation is required.

COPPER (Cu)

How common is it?

Cu deficiency is rare.

Symptoms

Cu deficiency first appears in young leaves that exhibit necrosis and coppery, bluish or gray with metallic sheen coloring at the tips and margins. The young leaves turn yellow between the veins.

Other symptoms include limp leaves that turn under at the edges and eventually die and wilting of the whole plant. New growth has difficulty opening, flowers do not mature or open in males and the stigmas don't grow properly.

Copper toxicity is rare but fatal. As the plant approaches death, its leaves yellow from its inability to use Iron (Fe). The roots are abnormally sized, then start to decay.

Mobility

Cu has low mobility.

Geoflora Nutrients VEG and BLOOM formulas are a balanced blend of 19 of organic inputs formulated to provide the optimal amounts of macronutrients, micronutrients and trace elements in a dustless, easy-to-apply granule. The granules also include yucca saponins, molasses, kelp and alfalfa, humates, crustacean meal, neem meal and beneficial bacteria that help the fertilizer percolate into the soil.

Role in plant nutrition

Cu is essential to healthy plant production, reproduction and maturity, and assists in carbohydrate metabolism and oxygen reduction.

Problem Solving

Foliar feeding with Cu fungicides such as Cu sulfate ($CuSO_4$) and chelated Cu alleviates deficiencies. Hydroponic and agricultural micronutrient formulas containing Cu also work. Compost, greensand and kelp concentrates are good natural sources.

General discussion

Cu deficiency is often confused with overfertilization.

Iron deficiency   Photo by Mel Frank

IRON (Fe)

How common is it?
Fe deficiency occasionally occurs outdoors, in planting mediums and in hydro.

Symptoms
Fe deficiency starts in new leaves, which lack chlorophyll and may have necrotic spots. This causes them to turn bright yellow except for the veins, which remain green. New leaves start to experience chlorotic molting, first near the base of the leaflets, so the middle of the leaf appears to have a brown mark. The veins remain dark green. Fe deficiency affects the new growth but not the lower leaves.

Mobility
Fe moves slowly in the plant.

Role in plant nutrition
Fe is necessary for enzymes to function and acts as a catalyst for the synthesis of chlorophyll. Young actively growing tissues need Fe to function. Older leaves also require a small supply.

To enhance plant nutrient absorption, optimize plant function and facilitate greater results with fewer nutrients, Nourish-L made with rare earth humates are a liquid conditioner derived from decomposed organic humus, natural marine animal carbon and cypress lignin. It can be used with your regular nutrient and fertilizer program.

Problem Solving

Fe deficiency may indicate a pH imbalance. Foliar-feed with Fe-chelated fertilizer containing Fe, Zn and Mn, since these deficiencies are often found in combination. Other Fe-bearing supplements include compost, Fe chelates (often found in hydroponic micronutrient supplements) and iron oxides (Fe_2O_3, FeO), for fast absorption. Supplements should be added both foliarly and to the planting medium. Adding rusty water also works.

General Discussion

Fe deficiency is often found in combination with Zn and Mn deficiencies. Fe deficiency may indicate that

Photo by Shadow

iron in the nutrient solution or media has combined with another nutrient such as a sulfate ion. This creates a solid salt that precipitates out of solution making the Fe unavailable. Adjust pH to resolve.

Magneium deficiency

MAGNESIUM (Mg)

How common is it?

Magnesium (Mg) deficiency is common in all mediums and hydro. It is not common outdoors.

Symptoms

Mg deficiency starts in the older leaves. The veins remain green while the rest of the leaf turns yellow, exhibiting chlorosis. The leaves eventually curl up and then die. The edges of affected leaves feel dry and crispy. As the deficiency continues it moves from the middle to upper leaves. Eventually the growing shoots change from a pale green to white. The deficiency is quite apparent in the upper leaves. At the same time, the stems and petioles turn purple.

Mobility

Mg is mobile.

Toxicity

Very high rates of Mg must be present to create any toxicity. Too much Mg causes the leaves to turn a dark green and growth to slow.

Role in plant nutrition

Mg helps support healthy veins and maintains leaf production and structure. It's required for chlorophyll production and enzyme breakdowns.

Problem Solving

Water-soluble nutrients containing Mg fix the deficiency. Such nutrients include Magnesium Sulfate ($MgSO_4$, Epsom salts) and Ca-Mg for fast absorption and dolomite lime/garden lime and worm castings for moderate absorption.

In hydro and planting mixes, Mg deficiency is easily fixed using 1 teaspoon of Epsom salts per gallon of water in reservoirs or when moistening the planting mix. After the first treatment, treat with one-quarter dose with each watering or change of reservoir. Calcium-Magnesium can also be used.

For fastest action, Epsom salts can be used foliarly at the rate of 1 teaspoon per gallon. Ca-Mg can be used foliarly as directed.

Dolomitic limestone contains large amounts of Magnesium. It can be used to raise the pH of soils and planting mixes and supply Magnesium at the same time.

General Discussion

Magnesium deficiency is one of the easiest nutrient deficiencies to diagnose and cure. It occurs more frequently if using distilled, rain, runoff, reverse osmosis or tap water that has low ppm count.

Both municipal water and well water contain magnesium. Municipal water generally has low levels of 5-20 ppm. Well water can have levels approaching 100 ppm, which is well above the 50 ppm delivered by many commercial hydroponic fertilizers. Cannabis probably needs a higher percentage, perhaps 100-150 ppm in hydroponic solutions for it to thrive.

$MGSO_4 = 20\%$ Mg

MANGANESE (Mn)

How common is it?
Mn deficiency is rare and almost always associated with Fe and Zn deficiencies.

Symptoms
Mn is immobile so deficiencies appear first at new growth while older leaves remain healthy looking. The leaf tissues turn yellow and small areas of tan/brown dead tissue (necrotic areas) appear in the middle of the leaf. The leaf veins usually stay green. The leaf becomes outlined in a ring of dark green along its margins. Too much Mn in the soil causes an Fe deficiency. The plant shows a lack of vigor.

Mobility
Manganese is not mobile.

Role in plant nutrition
Mn helps enzymes break down for chlorophyll and photosynthesis production, and it aids in making nitrates available for protein production.

Problem Solving
For fast relief, foliar-feed with a water-soluble fertilizer high in Mn such as $MnSO4$, Fe-Zn-Mn fertilizer, hydro micros or Mn chelate. Then add the fertilizer to the water/nutrient mix. Compost and greensand also contain Mn, but they are absorbed more slowly than the water solubles.

Fed from a diet of organic materials of crab shell, rock dust, humate, and coffee grounds, Premium Worm Castings are full of soil bacteria, chitinase, and fungus that make nutrients more available to roots, protect from insects and nourish soil bacteria.

MOLYBDENUM (Mo)

Molybdenum deficiency

How common is it?

Mo deficiency is very rare but is more likely to occur in color-changing strains in cold temperatures.

Symptoms

Mo is immobile so deficiencies appear first on new growth while older leaves remain healthy looking. The middle and lower leaves turn yellow. The leaf veins stay green. As the deficiency progresses toward the shoots the new leaves become distorted or twisted. Mo deficiency causes leaves to turn pale green, along with retarded or strange-looking leaf growth. Older chlorotic leaves experience rolled margins, stunted growth and red tips that move inward toward the middle of the leaves.

Sometimes Mo deficiency is misdiagnosed as N deficiency. However, N affects the bottom leaves first. Mo affects leaves in the middle of the plant first and then moves up to the newer growth.

Excessive Mo in cannabis looks like Fe or Cu deficiency.

Mobility

Mo is mobile.

Role in plant nutrition

Mo is contained in enzymes that help plants convert nitrates to ammonia, which is required for protein production.

Molybendum deficiency

Problem Solving

Foliar spraying with water-soluble fertilizers aids in overcoming the deficiency. Because plants need Mo in such extremely small amounts, a hydroponic micronutrient mix is often the most efficient way of supplying it. In addition to their use in hydroponic nutrient solutions, these fertilizers can be used as foliar sprays or applied to the soil.

General Discussion

Generally, Mo deficiency occurs when S and P are deficient. Mo toxicity does not tend to wreak havoc on plants, but excess intake causes severe problems in humans so extra precautions should be taken when using it.

NICKEL (Ni)

No Ni deficiency has been observed under crop-growing conditions, but in crop research settings, agricultural scientists have reproduced deficiency symptoms such as chlorosis of young leaves and dead meristematic tissue.

Stages of Nitrogen deficiency   Photo by Mel Frank

NITROGEN (N)

How common is it?

N deficiency is the most commonly occurring nutrient deficiency in cannabis.

Symptoms

N is a mobile nutrient so deficiency symptoms appear in lower leaves while new growth remains healthy. The leaves yellow and die as the N translocates to support new growth. Eventually the deficiency travels up the plant until only the new growth is green, leaving the lowest leaves to yellow and wither. Lower leaves die from the leaf tips inward.

Other symptoms include smaller leaves, slow growth and a sparse profile. The stems and petioles turn a red/purple tinge.

Too much N causes a lush dark green growth that is more susceptible to insects and disease. The stalks become brittle and break from lack of flexibility.

Mobility

N can travel anywhere on the plant. Usually deficiency starts on the lower of the plant because N travels to new growth.

Toxicity

Plants need large amounts of N during the vegetative stage. So much so, that it is often difficult to feed them too much. As the plants begin flowering, they require less N. See below for a general discussion on N levels throughout the life cycle. Some clear signs of N toxicity are: dark green leaves and curling of leaf tips, sometimes referred to as "clawing."

Role in plant nutrition

N is directly responsible for the production of chlorophyll and amino acids, and it is essential to photosynthesis. It is an essential element of tissue; without it, growth quickly stops.

Reiziger Grow Food A & B is a 2-part nutrient system that gives the most vigorous growth rates possible, was formulated for Dutch hydroponic master gardens and has been used for over thirty years.

Any water-soluble N (especially nitrates, NO_3) is readily available to the roots. Insoluble N, such as urea, needs to be broken down by microbes in the soil before the roots can absorb it. After fertilization, nitrogen-deficient plants absorb N as soon as it is available and start to change from pale to a healthy-looking Kelly green. Deficient plants usually recover in about a week, but the most-affected leaves do not recover.

N is the first number of the three-number set found on all fertilizer packages, which list N-P-K always in that order. Any water-soluble fertilizer much higher in N than P and K can be used to solve N deficiencies very quickly. Most hydro "Vegetative formulas" fall into this category.

The plant's lower leaves yellow and die as Nitrogen moves to the upper leaves.

Calcium nitrate ($CaNO_3$) is water-soluble and fast-acting. It can be used as a foliar fertilizer and in the water/nutrient solution.

Urea and urine, fish emulsion (5-1-1) and high-N bat or seabird guano also act quickly. High-N fertilizers such as alfalfa and cottonseed meals, manure, feather meal and fish meal all supply Nitrogen in soils but release it over the growing season.

General Discussion

Without high amounts of N, especially during the vegetative growth stage, the plant's yield is greatly reduced. Water uptake slows from lower photosynthesis due to lower production of chlorophyll. N issues happen throughout the entire growth cycle. Plants should never experience N deficiency during vegetative growth. However, overfertilizing with N causes problems too.

Tapering off the use of nitrogen towards flowering promotes flowering rather than vegetative growth. However, a small amount of N is always necessary in order for the plant to manufacture amino acids, which use N as an ingredient. This supports flower growth and utilization of P and K. Some "Bloom Boosters" have N-P-K ratios of "0-50-30." While high numbers sound impressive, using this fertilizer too early causes the flowers to be smaller than they could have been. If there is not enough residual N available, the plants are not getting the most out of the fertilizer.

In the middle to the end of the flowering stage, plants frequently show a N deficiency. They're using the nutrients that were stored in the leaves and dropping their oldest, bottom fan leaves. To prevent the deficiency from getting extreme, you can supplement nitrogen from a fast-acting source at a small or controlled rate, especially if the fertilizer flowering formula lacks N.

Phosphorous deficiency

PHOSPHORUS (P)

How common is it?

Because cannabis nutrient recipes use very high phosphorus levels, phosphorus deficiency is highly unlikely.

Symptoms

P is mobile so it moves from older leaves to new growth when there is a deficiency, so symptoms appear first on older leaves. First the leaves turn dark green and become weak. Then they develop dull blue or purple hues. The edges of the leaves turn tan/brown and curl downward as the deficiency works its way inward. The lower leaves turn yellow and die. This purpling can also be seen on stems and branches exposed to cool/cold temperatures.

The stems and petioles turn purple or red. Some strains, however, normally possess red or purple stems and petioles, so these traits are not a surefire sign of phosphorus deficiency. Plants exposed to cold conditions outside or frequent indoor temperature drops over 15°F can also exhibit these symptoms. Adverse cold conditions seem to adversely affect P uptake or availability

Plants use high amounts of P during flowering. Without abundant supplies, yields suffer.

Mobility
Phosphorus is mobile.

Role in plant nutrition
P aids in root and stem growth, influences the vigor of the plant and helps seedlings germinate. P is extremely important in the reproductive stages and flowering.

Problem Solving
P is the second number of the three-number ratio listed on fertilizer packages. Fast-acting fertilizers that fix the deficiency include water-soluble fertilizers containing high P such as high-P bloom fertilizers and the water soluble Monopotassium Phosphate MKP—1 gram dissolved in 1 gallon delivers 60 ppm of P and 76 ppm of K. Dilute this concentrate by 3 before serving it to the plants.

High-P guanos also provide readily available P. Rock phosphate and greensand are also high in P, but they release it gradually.

Affected leaves do not recover, but new growth is healthy.

General Discussion
Deficiency during flowering results in lower yields, but overfertilizing can result in "chemical buds" and "sparking buds" and "burnt leaves." Cold weather (below 50°F/10°C) interferes with P absorption. For this reason, soluble P such as found in water-soluble bloom formulas can add flower yield in cool weather.

P, along with K, accelerates the plant's metabolism during flowering. Vegetative plants require relatively low levels of P, about 20-30% of N levels. However, flowering plants react to high levels of P by radically ramping up the plant's growth. Flowering levels of P are often 10 times the vegetative levels and twice the N levels. P levels are usually ramped up immediately following transition and kept high until flushing.

Potassium deficiency Photo by Kristen Angelo

POTASSIUM (K)

How common is it?

K deficiency is highly uncommon when using commercial premixed nutrients and water-soluble nutrients.

Outdoors, light sandy and organic soils without much clay may be deficient in K because it is water soluble and can leach from the soil with heavy rains.

Symptoms

K is a mobile nutrient so it can be moved from older leaves to new growth. K deficiency shows up first on older leaves while new leaves remain healthy.

Plants suffering from minor deficiencies look vigorous, even taller than the rest of the population, but the tips and edges of their bottom leaves die or turn tan/brown and develop necrotic spots.

As the deficiency gets more severe the leaves develop chlorotic spots. Mottled patches of red and yellow appear between the veins, which remain green, accompanied by red stems and petioles. More severe deficiencies result in slower growth, especially when plants are in the vegetative stage. Severe K shortages cause leaves to grow smaller than usual.

Larger fan leaves have some dead patches, or necrosis, on their margins. These leaves eventually turn brown and die off.

Mobility
K is mobile.

Role in plant nutrition
K is necessary for all activities having to do with water transportation, as well as all stages of growth; it's especially important in the development of buds. K aids in creating sturdy and thick stems, disease resistance, water respiration and photosynthesis.

K, along with P, accelerates plant growth when added during flowering. Vegetative plants need K levels about equal to N levels. However, flowering plants react to high levels of K by ramping up metabolism and growth. Successful flowering levels of K are up to four times those of N.

Problem Solving
Although symptoms of minor K deficiency affect the cosmetic look of the plant, it does not seem to affect plant growth or yields. High levels of P and K are required in flower and all commercial premixed fertilizers, which deliver them in levels unheard of in mainstream

agriculture. In the very unlikely event you have K deficiency during flowering, yields will suffer dramatically!

Water-soluble fertilizers containing high K fix the deficiency. Bloom fertilizer contains high K levels. Wood ashes deliver K quickly. In addition to its nutrient value, it's highly alkaline K.

Fast-acting fertilizers

Potassium Nitrate (KNO_3): 1 gram in 1 gallon delivers 102 ppm of K and 37 ppm of N.

Potassium Sulfate (SO_4): 1 gram in 1 gallon delivers 119 ppm of K and 48 ppm of sulfur.

Mono Potassium Phosphate (MKP): 1 gram in 1gallon delivers 76 ppm of K and 60 ppm of P.

KSiO3 Potassium Silicate (K_2SiO_3): can be used to supply Si and contains 3% K.

Potassium di-hydrogen phosphate (KH_2PO_4).

Kelp contains organics and 3% K is moderately fast-acting.

Slow-release fertilizers:

Greensand

Granite dust

Slow release fertilizers take more time to get to the plant and are not usually used to correct deficiencies, but to prevent them. They should be used for amending soil over the long term.

Damaged leaves never recover, but the plant shows recovery in four to five days with applications of fast-acting products.

General Discussion

Cold weather slows K absorption, as does too much Ca or NH4+. High levels of Na displace K.

SILICON (Si)

How common is it?
Si is not an essential element to plants but it probably helps plants resist stresses. A lack of it does not cause any metabolic dysfunction and is likely totally undetectable.

Symptoms
There is no such thing as a Si deficiency. Plants grow well without it. However, when it is present there is some absorption. It seems to strengthen leaves, stems and perhaps roots. It also seems to make the plant less susceptible to fungal and bacterial diseases and insect infestation. The plant may also increase photosynthetic activity and increase overall yield.

Mobility
Si is not mobile.

Role in plant nutrition
Si helps the plant overcome different stresses that occur and helps to protect the plant from pests and diseases. It aids in growth, development, yield and disease resistance. It is used to strengthen stem and branch structure. Abundant amounts of Si may result in stronger stems and greater resistance to water stress. It helps plants resist pests by making the tissue tougher to pierce.

There are several ways to supply Si:
Diatomaceous earth is composed of the shells of diatoms. It can be added to planting mix.

Silica planting medium is composed of pebbles with a high composition of silica. It can be added to planting mix or used as a hydroponic medium. Both of these mediums gradually dissolve, releasing the mineral. Neither lends itself to urgent corrective action.

Potassium silicate is available as a powder or as a dilute liquid. It supplies both K and Si.

General Discussion
Si is abundant in nature. Even with an abundance of Si available plants take only what they can use, so there is no threat of overdosing.

Sulfur deficiency

SULFUR (S)

How common is it?

S deficiency is rare. You are not likely to encounter it.

Symptoms

The first signs of S deficiency are yellowing, young leaves. Leaf growth is slow; leaves become brittle and narrower than usual and are small and mutated. Buds die off at the tops of flowering plants. Overall growth is stunted. Some S deficiencies may show orange and red tints rather than yellowing. In severe cases the veins of the growing shoots turn yellow with dead areas at the base of the leaf where the blades join. The stems become hard and thin and may be woody. They increase in length but not in diameter.

Mobility

Like Fe, S moves slowly in the plant. Warmer temperatures make S harder for the plant to absorb. But unlike Fe, S is distributed evenly throughout the plant, mainly in big fan leaves. S deficiency starts at the back of the leaves and creeps toward the middle.

Toxicity

Too much S stunts the plant and leaf size, and the leaves look brown and dead at the tips. An excess of S looks like salt damage: restricted growth and dark color damage. This is also rare.

Role in plant nutrition

S is essential during vegetative growth and plays an important role in root growth, chlorophyll supply and plant proteins.

Problem Solving

Both organic soils and inorganic fertilizers contain high levels of available S so plants are not likely to suffer from a lack of the element. However, a deficiency is easily solved using Epsom salts ($MgSO_4$). Water the plant with Epsom salts until the condition improves. Mix 1 teaspoon per gallon and apply both foliarly and to the irrigation water. Adding nutrients containing S fixes the deficiency. Mix at recommended strength to avoid nutrient burn. Any water-soluble fertilizer that uses sulfur such as ammonium sulfate ($(NH_4)_2SO_4$ and potassium sulfate (K_2SO_4) also works. Another source is elemental garden sulfur, but this takes longer to work.

Sulfur deficiency

Zinc deficiency Photo by Mel Frank

ZINC (Zn)

How common is it?
Zn deficiency occurs occasionally. It often occurs combined with Fe and Mn deficiencies.

Symptoms
Zinc deficiency is identifiable by radically twisted leaf blades on new growth, chlorosis and yellowing between the veins of older leaves. Interveinal yellowing is often accompanied by overall paleness. During the flowering stage, buds may contort, twist and turn hard. When the deficiency first appears, the spotting can resemble that of Fe or Mn deficiency, but it affects new growth.

Zn excess is very rare but produces wilting and even death in extreme cases.

Mobility
Zn is not mobile in plants, so symptoms occur mainly in the newer growth.

From seedlings and cuttings to Grow Phase to Bloom, use SNS Perfect Mix Nutrients. Natural ingredients deliver the right amount of carefully blended nutrients and extra amino acids to grow strong healthy plants.

Role in plant nutrition

Zn aids in plant size and maturity, as well as in the production of leaves, stalks, stems and branches. Zn is an essential component in many enzymes and in the growth hormone auxin. Low auxin levels cause stunted leaves and shoots. Zinc is also important in the formation and activity of chlorophyll. Plants with high levels of zinc can tolerate longer droughts.

Problem Solving

Use an Fe-Zn-Mn micro mix to solve the deficiency. Zinc sulfate ($ZnSO4$), chelated Zn and zinc oxide (ZnO) also adjust the deficiency.

General Discussion

With low levels of Zn in the plants, yields are dramatically reduced.

Note: Zn, Fe and Mn get locked out when the pH is too high. These deficiencies often occur together.

Aphids   Photo by W. Cranshaw, CSU, Bugwood.org

Section 2

PESTS

Pests in the garden are among the most annoying and difficult problems. No matter the growing method, pests can infect the garden. Pests travel on clothes and pets. This is a good reason not to allow animals in the grow room. Additionally, pests can also arrive on the wind, though no fault of people or pets.

Make sure that the planting mix is composed of inert or pasteurized ingredients. Planting mix that is not sterile or pasteurized can contain bugs.

The larger an insect infestation, the harder it is to eradicate, and, greater the chances that it includes pests that are resistant to chemical warfare.

This section provides information that allows you to recognize and eradicate pests that affect Cannabis plants. As with the nutrients, the pests are listed in alphabetical order, but the ones that are most likely to attack cannabis are aphids; fungus gnats; mealybugs; scale; broad, russet, spider and hemp mites; and whiteflies.

A description of each pest is provided so that you can detect it and the damage it does. Preventive and control methods are provided to keep the pest away from the plants and get rid of an infestation.

ANTS

How common are they?

Ants are abundant both indoors and outdoors. Most of the species that affect marijuana use it for grazing their herds of aphids and mealybugs.

What does the pest look like?

Ants are made up of three main body parts: the head, thorax and abdomen. All six legs are attached to the thorax. The eyes and the jaw and antennae are connected to the head. Ants are generally quite small, usually only about 0.1 to 0.2 inch (about 2 to 5 mm) long. While sexually reproductive ants have wings, the worker ants do not. The worker ants will be the ones you are most likely to see in your garden.

Where is the pest found?

Ants can be found in the soil or planting medium, where they nest. They climb the stalk and graze their herds of aphids and mealybugs on the leaves.

What does it do to the plant?

They make their homes in underground colonies and must burrow to travel, thus causing damage to roots and root hairs. The aphids and mealybugs they herd are severe threats to plants because they suck vital juices and are vectors for disease.

General Discussion

Ants are attracted to plants that already have aphids, whiteflies, mealybugs and scale. Then they take these pests to new grazing areas. First they spread out on the plant and then move the herd to new plants. They will defend the herd from predators and parasitoids like ladybugs and parasitoid wasps. They hang out (in moving streams) on the plant and in and around the soil/medium.

Aphids, mealybugs and whiteflies secrete a sticky substance known as "honeydew," which consists of a sugar concentrate made from the plant's sap. Ants adore this honeydew, but this sticky annoyance causes sooty mold. Even if the plants do not have infestations of other pests, it is important to exterminate ants because of their ability to carry pests to the plants.

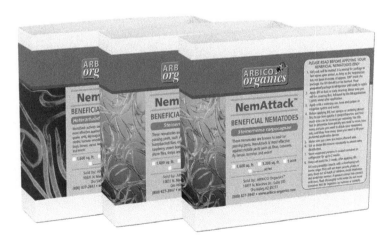

Depending on the pests trying to be controlled, select one or more species of beneficial nematodes. ARBICO Organics offers a large variety of nematodes, including Heterorhabditis bacteriophora, Steinernema feltiae and Steinernema carpocapsae. Mixed with water applied into the soil, applications should ideally be done twice yearly, in spring and in fall before pests overwinter.

Reproduction rate and life cycle: Ants are social creatures, living in colonies of queens and supported by workers. Some species have only one queen per colony, while others may have several. The adult's life cycle begins with an egg laid by a queen, then progresses through a larval stage, a pupal stage and finally to adulthood. In many species only the oldest adults work outside the colony, while 90% of the ants work in the nest. Colonies reproduce when a newly hatched queen selects several males and either walks or flies to a new location.

Ants regulate their reproductive rates depending on conditions in the colony and the outside environment. They do this partly by varying the length of the pupal stage and partly by selecting certain larvae or pupae to be transformed into queens and drones. If weather is suitable and there is ample food and water for the size of the colony, they will reproduce faster, then slow down reproduction when conditions become less favorable. What this means to the gardener is that it is not enough to destroy only the ants you see. You need to eliminate the colony itself because lost workers are rapidly replaced.

Prevention

There are many ways to deter ants from wandering into the grow area and getting to the plants.

- Moats: Most ants don't swim so a moat prevents them from crawling from the floor or table to the container. A simple moat can be made using a wide tray and a support such as a thick piece of Styrofoam or a block of wood. Place the plant container on top of the support. Fill the tray with water. However, some species find ways to cross barriers.
- Herbal barrier: Ants are repulsed by cinnamon, cloves and bay leaves. Pour the ground spice in a perimeter around the garden. Ants will not cross it. Brew a tea from these spices and spray it around the plants to repulse the pests.
- Chemical barriers: Boric acid, which is sometimes used as an eyewash, also can be used as a barrier. Occasionally, ants cross this barrier, but they become coated with the powder, which slowly kills them. In addition, they carry the poison back to the nest.
- Diatomaceous earth, the skeletons of minute sea animals, is mined and ground into a fine powder. It is often used in swimming pool filters. When used as a barrier and kept dry, it kills insects with its sharp points, which puncture insects crawling over it.

- Sticky paper: Sticky cards or flypaper can be used as a perimeter barrier or the stem can be banded with the stick-um. Don't apply it directly to the stem. Wrap paper around the stem and then apply the sticky substance to the paper. It is an easy, nontoxic solution to ants that works well. Two products that are designed for this are sticky traps and Tanglefoot, which is a stick-um that can be spread on surfaces.
- A product called Venerate XC contains heat-killed Burkholderia spp and is highly effective against ants. This is a kill on contact poison and must be applied to the living ants. There is no residual control once the product has dried.

Control

- Spices: Use a cinnamon-clove tea to flush ants from planting mediums. When the dry powder is placed on the soil, the ants start vacating the premises. Other natural substances that are repulsive to ants include cayenne pepper, citric extracts, mint extracts, cream of tartar and some mints and sages.
- Boric acid baits: Ants are interested in either grease and oil or sugars. Most ants that bother plants are sugar lovers. Sweets and fats can be mixed with boric acid to make a toxic ant lunch. See the control section for recipes.
- Pyrethrum: Pyrethrum is a natural plant protector harvested from a chrysanthemum family plant. It is lethal to ants and other insects, including pollinators. It is available as powders and sprays. Please follow the instructions on the bottle for application as these pesticides can be harmful to humans and pets when used incorrectly.

  Currently, cannabis producers cannot use pyrethrum products in regulated states because of the presence of piperonyl butoxide (PBO) in most pyrethrum products. PBO shows up in trace amounts in subsequent harvests of cannabis produced in the same location.
- Commercial ant baits and stakes use minute amounts of poison to kill ants and carry the toxic substances back to the nest. Many brands are available. Don't place these in the soil. Instead make sure the ants' path crosses these baits.

Aphids in multiple life stages   Photo by W. Cranshaw, CSU, Bugwood.org

APHIDS

How common are they?

Aphids are a common pest.

What does the pest look like?

Aphids are small, pear-shaped soft-bodied insects about 1 to 3 mm long. Like all insects, they have six legs, a pair of antenna, and three body segments: head, thorax and abdomen. There are thousands of species that vary in color from green to yellow, black or brown. Some have wings, some are covered with wax or "wool" made from webbing they secrete and others have unique distinguishing features.

Common to all aphids, distinguishing them from all other insects, are a pair of "cornicles" which extend like tailpipes from their abdomen. These can vary in length and color.

Where is the pest found?

Aphids colonize the stems and undersides of plant leaves. Some species, such as the black bean aphid, are quite noticeable because their color stands out from the plant. Others, such as the green peach aphid, are often colored spring green and blend in with young leaves.

What does it do to the plant?

Aphids are true bugs. Like all bugs, they live on plant juices by puncturing leaves using a straw-like mouth called a proboscis to suck sap from stems, branches and leaves. In order to obtain enough protein, aphids suck a lot of juice, extract the protein and excrete the concentrated sugar solution that is referred to as "honeydew." The aphid excrement attracts ants that herd the suckers, protecting them from predators. Honeydew is a growth medium for sooty fungus, which causes necrosis of leaf parts.

Aphid   Photo by W. Cranshaw, CSU, Bugwood.org

Heavy aphid infestations cause leaf curl, wilting, stunting of shoot growth and delay in production of flowers and fruit, as well as a general decline in plant vigor.

Aphids are vectors for hundreds of diseases and can quickly cause an epidemic. They transfer viruses, bacteria and fungi from plant to plant.

General Discussion

Aphids are true "bugs," sucking insects in the order Hemiptera. Most aphid species have a complex life cycle. Many species overwinter as eggs, but during most of the season they are nonsexual and deliver nymphs pathogenically. These nymphs are live-birthed and born pregnant. A single species produces populations that differ depending on the season. For instance, seasonally, when infestations become dense, some populations have wings and colonize new plants by traveling on air currents. Each live-birth generation exists for only 7 to 14 days. If left unchecked, aphid populations rapidly grow to thousands.

SoluNeem is NOT neem oil. A highly concentrated, organic water soluble neem powder, SoluNeem needs no emulsifiers or detergents and can cover 1,000 sq ft with one tsp in one gallon of water OMRI certified organic, SoluNeem leaves no sticky residue while eliminating aphids, thrips, white flies, caterpillars, and more. Use as a foliar spray as well as root drench in irrigation and hydroponics up to the day of harvest with no phytotoxicity.

Sexual populations appear in the fall, resulting in eggs that overwinter. All species have temperature-dependent rates of reproduction. But even at the same temperature, aphids may reproduce at different rates based on nutrition from the host plant.

Most aphids live only in the plant canopy. Root aphids, most commonly the rice root aphid, live in the planting medium and feed on the roots, making early detection and treatment much more difficult.

Indoors, with no predators to keep them in check, aphids can overrun a garden in short order.

Prevention

Air Filtration: Aphids are airborne for part of their life cycle. Use a 340 micron mesh or filter to keep them out of the grow space. A thrips screen should be used in the garden. It works on aphids as well.

Monitoring: Check the plants regularly for aphids—at least twice weekly when plants are growing rapidly. Most species of aphids cause the greatest damage when temperatures are warm but not hot (65-80°F). Inspect root zones and around the tops of pots for aphids in the media. Shaking a container can dislodge some aphids from bottom of the container. Use this technique to spot occurrence.

Catch infestations early. Once their numbers are high and they have begun to distort and curl leaves, aphids are hard to control because the curled leaves shelter them from insecticides and natural enemies.

Aphids tend to be most prevalent along the upwind edge of the garden and close to other sources of aphids, so make a special effort to check these areas. Many aphid species prefer the undersides of leaves, or tender terminating stalks, so check there.

Aphids usually feed on the underside of leaves or on stems. Colors include black, green and red. Once aphid infestation is identified, investigate its extent, then treat aggressively. Dead aphids leave white remains of their exoskeletons. These are sometimes mistaken for other organisms.

Outdoors, check for evidence of natural enemies such as lady beetles, lacewings, syrphid fly larvae and the mummified skins of parasitized aphids. Look for disease-killed aphids as well: they may appear off-color, bloated, flattened or moldy. These observations should be considered when evaluating treatment strategies. Substantial numbers of these natural control factors can mean that the aphid population may be reduced rapidly without the need for treatment.

Aphids

Photos by W. Cranshaw, CSU, Bugwood.org

Some species of ants farm aphids, carrying them to fresh grazing areas and protecting them from predators. They collect the honeydew, the concentrated sap excreted by the aphids. If you notice ants in the picture, you will have to control to control the aphids.

Control

Sometimes aphids must be controlled outdoors. Often this can be accomplished by spraying them off with water. Spraying several days apart will knock down the population considerably, reducing plant stress. If aphids remain a problem, consider one of the controls listed in the indoor section. Check for ants: when they are present aphids are much more difficult to control, so they must also be eliminated.

Control over 300 insect species with AzaGuard. Labelled for drench and foliar applications to target pests such as root aphids, fungus gnats, mites and thrips. AzaGuard's food grade, no residue formula is an ideal solution for your garden. OMRI Listed for organic production.

Indoor Aphid Control

Indoors and in the greenhouse aphids have an easy life. Without threats from weather and by living in a relatively predator-free area, they don't suffer losses to these relentless killers. Without the pitfalls they suffer in nature, aphid population growth reaches exponential proportions quickly.

Since the balance of nature isn't operative indoors, the gardener must intervene before an outbreak has reached epic proportions. There are a lot of choices:

Aphid Parasitoids: Professionals often use parasitoids when there is an outbreak that hasn't reached epic proportions. Predators are recommended for heavy infestations. However, this may reflect profressionals' preference for aggressive predators over subtle parasites. The predators spend a portion of their life eating aphids, and close-up their actions can be as vicious and dramatic as an alligator's.

The parasitoids inject an egg into the aphid. The egg hatches and the parasitoid larvae feast inside. Most aphids die within one to two hours of this egg-laying. The body of the aphid undergoes a dramatic change as it becomes a "mummy" changes color and bloats. Each larva emerges as an adult *Alien*-style from the mummy. Not

Aphid leaf damage

71

quite as dramatic, except when the adult crawls out of the corpse, but every bit as effective. The old mummy remains stay on the leaf.

Among the most important natural enemies are various species of parasitoid wasps (such as *Aphidius colemani*, *Aphidius matricariae* and *Aphidius ervi*) that lay their eggs inside aphids. The generation time of most parasitoid wasps is quite short when the weather is warm, so once mummies begin to appear on the plants, the aphid population is likely to be reduced substantially within a week or two. These wasps are tiny and do not have stingers so they pose no threat to people or pets.

Many predators also feed on aphids. The most well known are the common lady beetle (*Hippodamia convergens*), green lacewing (*Chrysopa rufilabris*) and predatory flies (*Aphidoletes aphidimyza*, Aphidius colemani, Aphelinus abdominalis, Aphidius ervi). Naturally occurring predators work best, especially in small backyards. Commercially available lady beetles may give some temporary control when properly handled, although most of them disperse away from the yard within a few days. They are most effective in protecting large areas rather than small plots, which they are likely to leave in search of dense prey infestations.

Aphids are very susceptible to fungal diseases when it is humid. Whole colonies of aphids can be killed by these pathogens when conditions are right. Look for dead aphids that have turned reddish or brown; they have a fuzzy, shriveled texture unlike the shiny, bloated, tan-colored mummies that form when aphids are parasitized. Make a pesticide by taking these dead aphids, blending them with water (1-3 teaspoons of aphids per quart) and spraying the solution on plants.

- *Beauveria bassiana* (beneficial fungi)
- Capsaicin
- Carbon dioxide
- Cinnamon oil
- Cloves
- Coriander oil
- Garlic
- Horticultural oil
- Insecticidal soap
- Neem oil
- Peppermint oil
- Pyrethrum
- Soap
- Vacuuming

Photo by W. Cranshaw, CSU, Bugwood.org

CATERPILLARS (CUTWORMS, CABBAGE WORMS, LEAF-EATERS, CORN BORERS)

How common are they?

In spring and summer, caterpillars are common outdoors but rare indoors.

What does the pest look like?

Caterpillars are the larval stage of butterflies and moths. They have soft, segmented bodies with a head, thorax and abdomen. The thorax contains three pairs of jointed legs that have hooks, and the abdomen has five pairs of stumpy legs. Caterpillars are often the same color as the leaves so they are hard to spot.

There are many species of caterpillars that feed on cannabis. They have different seasons of activity, rates of growth and developmental strategies that can make them more challenging depending on when and where cannabis is growing.

73

For example, "budworms" such as the tobacco budworm (*Helicoverpa armigera*) burrow into flower, often at an early stage, so they are very resistant to treatments that require direct contact. Sometimes called cutworms, armyworms, such as the fall armyworm (*Spodoptera frugiperda*), feed on foliage in a more conventional way but are known to "cut down" smaller plants early in their development. Finally, tortricid moth larvae are leaf eaters. They curl leaves with silk in order to feed and skeletonize nearby leaves. This also protects them against contact treatments.

Caterpillars that feed on cannabis are generalists. Eggs are laid on the foliage. When they hatch the larvae (caterpillars) feed on the plant and its nearby neighbors. Limiting access to the plants is easier inside a structure or by using row covers. The moths don't have easy access on the host plant to lay their eggs and the caterpillars are less likely to find access if they are crawling.

It's a good idea to familiarize yourself with the species that you observe so that you can prevent or treat future infestations.

In addition to this general outline, here are some specifics on the types of caterpillars that commonly infest cannabis:

Cabbage worms: Also called cabbage loopers. The adults are gray-brown moths with a wingspan of about 1.5 inches (4 cm). The caterpillars are green, usually with narrow white stripes along the body, and may grow up to 1.5 inches (3.75 cm) long. A distinctive feature of the cabbage-worm and other loopers are the way they move: arching its back to bring its hind legs forward, then extending its body. Eggs are ridged and dome-shaped and usually laid singly on the undersides of leaves.

Corn borers: The adults are yellow or tan-colored nocturnal moths with wingspans of about 1 inch (2.5 cm). The caterpillars are about 1 inch long; light brown in color with a brown head and spots on each segment. Eggs are white to pale yellow, laid in clusters of 20 to 30 on the undersides of leaves. As their name states, they often bore into the stalks. This destroys the liquid pathways, and all vegetation above the bore hole quickly wilts from dehydration.

Cutworms: The adults are gray to dark brown moths with wingspans of 1.25 to 1.75 inches (3 to 4.5 cm). The caterpillars grow to 1 to 1.5 inches (2.5 to 3.75 cm) long, plump and sturdy, ranging in color from brown to pink, green, gray and black. Eggs vary widely by species but are usually laid on the stems or the upper sides of leaves.

Leaf eaters: Many different species. The adults are usually moths, varying widely in color and with wingspans ranging from 1 to 1.75 inches (3 to 4.5 cm). The caterpillars are usually green but sometimes range from gray to brown, and are up to 1.5 inches (3.75 cm) long. Some leaf eaters are "wooly bear" caterpillars, their bodies covered with long hairs that look much like fur. The eggs may be found anywhere on the plant, depending on the species.

Photo by W. Cranshaw, CSU, Bugwood.org

Where the pests are found

Some caterpillars eat leaves. Others bore into the stem and eat the pith, the stem's soft inner tissue. Cutworms feed at night and spend the day in shallow burrows near the plants. Some caterpillars pupate in cocoons in the foliage, others move to the soil to pupate underground.

What do they do to the plant?

Caterpillars eat both leaves and the soft stems. Borers pierce the stem and eat the soft inner tissue. The branches and leaves above the caterpillar wilt, since they receive no water or nutrients. If it is a main stem, the whole plant dies. If it is a side stem, only that branch succumbs. In addition to the direct damage they cause, caterpillars leave behind damaged tissues that are more vulnerable to infections, especially gray mold.

How they work

Caterpillars are voracious eating machines and can savage plants very quickly. They chew continuously to support their high growth rate. Caterpillars can destroy a tray of seedlings overnight.

General Discussion

There are hundreds of species of caterpillar that attack cannabis. They vary widely in size, color, lifestyle and feeding habits. You'll know leaf-eaters and cabbage worms by the large holes that they leave in the plants' leaves. The size of the holes indicates caterpillar damage and not that of smaller pests. Cabbage worms also infest buds: a bud that turns brown and wilts may house a cabbage worm consuming it from within.

Cutworms are perhaps the most obvious of all caterpillars: Plants damaged by cutworms are literally chewed through at the soil line, causing the plant to topple. Seedlings and young plants are completely consumed.

Corn borers attack mature plants—they need a stem large enough to hold their bodies. They lay eggs in clusters on the leaves. After hatching, they eat the leaves around the eggs for two weeks to a month, leaving close clusters of tiny holes. To catch borers early, look for these small holes. Later in the season look for small holes in the plant stalks, possibly covered with thin silky webbing. After borers have been at work for a while, they sometimes cause the stalk to develop "fusiform galls." These are bulges in the plants' stalks that widen in the middle and taper at both ends. The borers may leave visible trails on the stalks leading to the galls.

Reproduction rate and life cycle: the moths and butterflies lay one or two batches of eggs each year, though some species may produce up to six generations per year in warm climates. Each female lays several hundred eggs. Depending on the species, they mate in spring to early summer, and the caterpillars emerge in the early summer to fall. They feed until they are ready to enter the pupal stage, when they spin cocoons or dig burrows and hibernate until they emerge as adult moths. Those species that emerge in late summer and fall often overwinter as caterpillars; emerging in early spring to begin feeding again (this is especially common with cutworm species).

In general, butterflies and moths reproduce slowly compared to many pests, but they have large appetites and a single caterpillar can cause a lot of damage.

Prevention

Because caterpillars vary so widely in their habits, the prevention methods vary widely as well. Planting indoors all but eliminates caterpillars. If you do plant outdoors, keep seedlings indoors as long as possible before transplanting, to prevent caterpillars from wiping them out. Clear the garden of weeds, grasses and plant debris throughout the year, but especially at the end of the growing season. Use electric "bug zappers" with blue or ultraviolet light to attract and destroy nocturnal moths. Tilling before planting brings caterpillars to the surface where they are eaten by birds and other predators.

Use netting or screening to cover outdoor plants. Make sure the screen is small enough to prevent moths from dropping eggs.

Cabbage worms: Use row covers in spring, when the adult moths breed, to prevent them from laying eggs on the plants.

Corn borers: Destroy stalks and other plant debris after harvest.

Cutworms: Plant seedlings as large as possible. Turn the upper 2 inches of soil two weeks before planting and destroy any larvae you find. Put a "cutworm barrier" around each seedling. Easy to make is a metal can with top and bottom removed. Place it around the seedling so it goes at least 1 inch (2.5 cm) into the soil and 4 inches (10 cm) above the soil.

Garlic: Repels egg-laying moths.

Leaf-eaters: Use row covers to block egg-laying adults. Wrap stems with aluminum foil above and below major branches and apply a layer of Tanglefoot or similar stick-um to the foil. These barriers block caterpillars moving along the stems. Turn the soil before planting, especially in the spring, to destroy overwintering larvae and pupae.

Control

Quite a few nontoxic and least-toxic methods can be used to eliminate caterpillars.

- If you have only a few plants, the easiest way to control caterpillars is by physically destroying them. If you spot cutworm damage, you can usually find the caterpillars within about 10 inches (25 cm) of the damaged plants.
- Raking the soil down to about 2 inches (5 cm) may uncover them.
- Shake them or handpick them from plants.
- Forcefully spray water from a hose.
- Use a a vacuum cleaner to remove them.
- BTK or BT is a living bacterium, *Bacillus thuringiensis*, which the caterpillars ingest. It is the most effective treatment for caterpillars and is allowed in most regulated cannabis states for production. The bacteria sicken caterpillars but are harmless to humans and pets and even adult butterflies and moths. Once the caterpillars ingest the germ, they stop

eating and die within a short time. As they die they release new generations of bacteria that are hungry for caterpillar. The insecticide should be used at the first sign of caterpillars. Sunlight degrades the bacteria so they will need to be applied more often in the height of summer to maintain full coverage.

- Capsaicin
- Cinnamon
- Insecticidal soaps
- Neem oil: Diluted neem oil can be sprayed on plants every 10 days. It makes them unappetizing to caterpillars. Direct hits can be toxic to the leaf-eaters.
- Pyrethrum without additives
- Soap
- Trichogramma wasps: Several species of tiny stingless wasps attack and destroy caterpillar eggs before they hatch. They must be released at the earliest sign of infestation and cannot be used with most insecticides (BT and Spinosad are exceptions). Consult the supplier for recommended species and coverage rates.
- *Caution:* Spinosad is not allowed in cannabis production in regulated states. It has been found to be highly toxic when combusted.

Special note on stem borers: If you do not control stem borers quickly, your yield will be greatly decreased or even nonexistent. Before they bore into the stalk, you can eliminate them using the same techniques as for caterpillars.

It is a different story once they are situated in the stem's enclosure. Sometimes you can yank the borers right out of the holes they've chewed. Another method is to bore a hole in the stem above the borer and inject one of the recommended caterpillar insecticides into the stem using either a syringe or an eyedropper.

Stem borer

Photo by W. Cranshaw, CSU, Bugwood.org

DEER

How common are they?

Deer populations vary widely, both geographically and by habitat. They favor light forest and grasslands near forested areas and dislike getting more than a few hundred yards from cover. Gardens in suburban areas built near forest often have problems with grazing deer. Garden plots set up in wild or rural areas are very likely to be visited by deer if the habitat supports them.

What does the pest look like?

Deer are grazers with graceful bodies, thin legs and long necks. They vary greatly in size depending on species, age and sex, but they usually fall between 4 feet and 6 feet (1.2 and 1.8 m) long and weigh 80 to 220 pounds (35 to 100 kg). Deer in southern areas are smaller than northern deer. The males carry antlers beginning in late summer, shedding them usually in very late winter through spring. Northern deer are heavier than southern deer.

Deer emerge from forest cover at night to browse on plants but flee quickly when approached. They have excellent senses so most of the time the gardener knows them only by their tracks and the damage they leave. However, deer that have become accustomed, or attenuated to humans often graze during the day.

What they do to the plant

Deer prefer fresh leaves, fruit and other rich plant matter. In the marijuana garden they strip plants of leaves and buds and even tear up small plants and eat them whole.

General discussion

Marijuana evolved cannabinoids in part as protection against herbivores. Most mammals find the leaves and flowers unpleasant. Deer are among the few exceptions. Deer may be attracted to your garden simply because it's a food supply that most other herbivores leave alone. They prefer young, tender plants. As marijuana plants mature and cannabinoid levels increase, deer find the plants less palatable.

Deer damage is fairly easy to spot. They lack upper incisor teeth so a deer takes hold of leaves with its lips and lower teeth, then tears them off. This creates ragged browse damage, very different from the neatly clipped leaves left by rodents. Also, look for deer tracks and droppings near the garden.

Reproduction rate and life cycle: Deer follow a normal mammalian life cycle. They mate in the late fall through midwinter, and the female gives birth to one or sometimes two fawns in late spring to early summer. Deer usually mature in one to two years and live for 10 to 20 years if not killed by predators or disease, usually about five years in the wild. Their life span in the wild is usually fewer than five years.

Prevention

Naturally, deer pose little threat to plants grown indoors. Any outdoor garden near deer habitat is vulnerable, however.

The only effective option to prevent deer damage is to keep them away from the plants. There are two main ways of doing this: repellents and fences. Repellents are less expensive and may be the only option if discretion is important. But fencing is more certain when it is practical.

Deer find the odors of garlic, capsaicin and rotten eggs offensive, and commercial repellents containing these ingredients are available under several brands.

Other materials also repel deer by smell:

- Anything that carries a human's scent, such as worn clothing or human urine.
- Urine or scat from dogs or other predators. Predator urine is available commercially. Scat is sometimes available from your local zoo.
- Scented bar soap, especially Dove suspended in a net bag near the plants.

If you are not certain that a repellent is safe for use on food plants, then surround the marijuana plants with other plants that you don't plan to eat. Replace the repellent according the manufacturer's instructions, or every few days for the other scent repellents listed above.

Scent isn't the only way to repel deer. Anything that startles or frightens them is effective. Buy several home motion detectors at a hardware store and set them up in a perimeter around the grow site. Depending on the resources at the site, motion detectors can be rigged to trigger high-pressure water sprinklers (these are sold as "scarecrow sprinklers"), bright lights, battery-powered radios or ultrasonic noise when a deer approaches. Remember to set up lights to point away from the plants.

A final word about repellents: Deer become attenuated to most sounds, sights or smells. Once they realize that the repellent isn't harming them, they learn to ignore it. To reduce attenuation, change the repellent regularly, not just from one brand to another, but by using different ingredients and/or methods. Combining methods is also useful. For example, setting up an odor repellent and a scarecrow sprinkler together.

Even with repellents, the chance of predation grows with water and food stress. Deer will choose sources where there is less stress. As food or water become stressed, deer will take more risks [to find it]. In that case the only way to protect the garden is to fence it.

Fencing must be constructed with the abilities and habits of deer in mind. A deer can jump any fence less than 8 feet (2.4 m) high, if it can get close enough. Fences must also be built tight to the ground, or deer can slip under them. One alternative to an 8-foot fence is an electrified fence. Deer prefer to slip through a barrier rather than jump over it if that looks possible. So a standard electric fence built from two or three strands of 20-gauge smooth wire on insulated posts often deters them. Once they try to slip between the strands and get shocked, they generally keep several feet away from the fence—too far for them to jump it. A variant called a "Minnesota fence" actually uses an attractive bait such as peanut butter to get the deer to lick the fence or a foil tag attached to the fence. The deer gets a mild shock and avoids the fence completely after that.

Control

There is no practical means of controlling deer, in the sense of eradicating them, and this would not be a good option even if there were such a means. The outdoor marijuana gardener should leave the deer's natural predators (mainly coyotes and wild dogs) alone, as these provide some check on the deer population. However, aside from that, prevention is your best choice.

Perimeter fencing is one method of controlling deer invasions.

Fungus gnat

FUNGUS GNATS

How common are they?

Fungus gnats are common indoors. They are found outdoors in moist warm areas.

What does the pest look like?

Fungus gnats are flies about 3-4 mm in size and dark grayish black. They have a slender build with delicate long legs, a small round head with long antenna and two long wings. They look similar to a mosquito. The maggots are clear to creamy white in color with a shiny black head and can be up to .25 inch (6 mm) long but are usually smaller. The most common ones, found in gardens and house plants are in the *Bradysia* species, known as dark winged fungus gnats.

Where the pest is found?

Adults fly close to the soil level and through the plant lower canopy. Fungus gnat larvae live at the root level, usually from 1 to 3 inches (2.5 to 7.5 cm) below the soil line. In shallow containers the maggots may be found wiggling in the drain tray after watering.

What it does to the plant?

Fungus gnats' maggots eat roots, root hairs and organic matter, which weakens the plant. They tunnel into the plant stem, causing the stem to collapse. The maggots are also vectors for various diseases such as Pythium, Fusarium and Verticillium. Adult fungus gnats do not have mouths. The live only to reproduce.

Fungus gnat larvae

General Discussion

Outdoors, adults and larvae live in moist, shady areas. The adults hover near the soil surface. The larvae live at the root level. Fungus gnat larvae attack plant roots growing in planting medium, rock wool and other planting media. Indoors, females are attracted to moist planting mix, including rockwool.

Reproduction rate and life cycle: The adult females lay eggs at the surface of moist soil, near the plant stem. The larvae hatch out in four to ten days, depending on temperature, and feed off fungus and plant matter (including plant roots), then pupate in the soil and emerge as adults. The total time from egg to reproductive adult is about four weeks, and each female may lay several hundred eggs in small batches. Indoors, they breed continuously throughout the year and reproduce very rapidly.

Fungus gnats, particularly those in the genus *Bradysia*, are very common pests to encounter. Despite their common name, larvae feed on both fungal and plant matter, and they can be vectors for several plant pathogens, including *Fusarium*. Fungus Gnats reproduce well in moist, organically rich substrates, and can sometimes be a sign of poor irrigation management, especially over watering.

Prevention

If plants are outdoors, check the soil for adult gnats or larvae before bringing them indoors.

Prevent indoor entry of gnats by keeping screens on all open windows. Place a barrier over the soil so the gnats have no place to lay their eggs. A piece of cloth, cardboard or a layer of sand all work.

Fungus gnats need moist soil near the surface to reproduce. Avoid overwatering soil and let the soil dry between watering as much as the plants will tolerate (usually to a depth of about 1 inch (2-3 cm). A layer of light, well-draining planting media ingredients such as sand, vermiculite, perlite, or diatomaceous earth at the top helps with this. This disrupts the larval gnats' food supply and makes it difficult for an infestation to take hold.

In hydroponic gardens, fungus gnats can be an issue for rockwool specifically. The green algae that likes to grow on rockwool that's exposed to light and moisture is an environment the gnats thrive in. To prevent its culture on your rockwool or any other media, cover it to remove the light. The algae need light to live. No algae, fewer gnats. Hydrogen peroxide at a 10-20% dilution can be used to clean the surface areas. A drench at 1% can be fed to infected root zones in dire measures.

Keeping the top of the growing substrate dry decreases the attraction and subsequent incidence of fungus gnats. This may simply require a strategic watering plan. Predatory soil mites like *Hypoaspis miles* or *Stratiolaelaps scimitus* are preventive biocontrol agents that can be established in the crop. The insect-killing fungus *Beauveria bassiana* can also be applied to growing substrates to help control populations.

Control
- *Bacillus thuringiensis* (beneficial bacteria)
- Barriers (coir covers, sand, cloth, cardboard, etc.)
- Cinnamon oil and tea
- Diatomaceous earth
- Horticultural oil
- Insecticidal soaps
- Media topping—vermiculite, perlite, diatomaceous earth
- Neem
- Potassium salts of fatty acids
- Predatory mites (*Hypoaspis* species)
- Predatory nematodes, S. Feltiae is the most effective species *Heterorhabditis* is also effective.
- Pyrethrum
- Any soil barriers

Gopher

GOPHERS

How common are they?

Gophers are a very occasional problem in the garden. They are found mainly in the central and western United States, in Florida, and in Mexico.

What does the pest look like?

Gophers are medium-size rodents ranging from about 5 to nearly 14 inches (13 to 36 cm) long (not including tail). Their fur is very fine and ranges in color from nearly black to pale brown. The forepaws have strong claws. The head is small and flattened, with small ears and eyes and very prominent incisor teeth.

Where the pest is found?

Gophers tunnel underneath gardens and lawns.

What they do to the plant

Gophers feed on plants in three ways:

1. They feed on roots that they encounter when digging their tunnels.
2. They may venture short distances (only a body length or so) from their tunnels to eat vegetation on the surface.
3. They pull vegetation into their tunnels from below.

Gophers are prey to badgers, which eat them. Badgers can cause considerable damage when digging for their food.

General Discussion

When gophers are suspected, the first task is to make sure that they aren't moles. Moles cause little direct damage to gardens, and as a result they're seldom worth the trouble to eradicate. It is rare to see either one on the surface, so the best way to distinguish them is by observing the signs they leave behind.

First, check their diggings: A molehill is usually a rough cone with a hole or an earthen "plug" near the center. A gopher mound is more fan-shaped, with the hole or plug near one edge.

Next, look for damage. Moles generally cause very little damage. Gophers may chew the plants' roots, causing them to wilt and making it possible to pull them up with just a slight tug. If plants are chewed off completely at the soil line, or completely gone, roots and all, then chances are good that there is a gopher problem.

Reproduction rate and life cycle: Gophers mate once a year, in the spring, and produce a litter of up to five young in late spring to early summer. They live for up to 12 years.

Prevention

Containers, indoor gardening and hydroponic systems offer complete protection against gophers. In the field minimize weeds, as they are likely to attract gophers. If you are planting directly in the soil, line the planting hole on the bottom and sides with hardware cloth. Anecdotal evidence suggests a border of oleander plants around your garden repels gophers. Any of several commercial gopher repellents (most include castor oil, garlic or capsaicin) placed in the mouth of the mound may drive them off.

Control

It is best to try repellents first, as they are by far the easiest way to deal with go-phers. However, sometimes the only solution is to eliminate them.

The simplest means of exterminating gophers is fumigation. However, this will poison the soil for marijuana cultivation so it should not be used. Do not use this method. Commercial fumigants are generally paper or cardboard cartridges filled with charcoal and potassium nitrate.

Carbon dioxide (CO_2) gassing is a safer method of fumigation. The simplest way of getting it into the gopher's tunnel is either direct from a CO_2 tank (place the delivery hose in the tunnel opening) or as dry ice. Drop 8 to 16 ounces (225 to 450 grams) of dry ice into the tunnel, or deliver a similar amount of CO_2 from the tank. Rather than poisoning, CO_2 suffocates the pests.

Fumigation is not always effective. If not, then trapping is the only way. Suit-able traps are available at garden shops, both box traps and lethal forms.

Water in and wipe out damaging insects with SNS-209™ Organic Systemic Pest Control. Made from 100% pure botanical extracts that are water soluble and food grade, it is FIFRA section 25(b) exempt.

Leaf miners

LEAF MINERS Adult: 1/12" • 2 mm

How common are they?

Leaf miners are not common in indoor marijuana gardens. Outdoors leaves are occasionally attacked, but they are not usually a threat to the plant or yield. The three most common are in the genus Liriomyza, commonly known as the pea leaf miner, the American leaf miner and the vegetable leaf miner.

What do the pests look like?

Leaf miners in cannabis are usually the larval form of various species of flies, though a few species of moths and beetles also produce leaf-mining larvae. These larvae are very small maggots—seldom more than 3 mm long—ranging in color from white to pale green. The adult flies resemble tiny houseflies, about 2 mm long.

Leaf miner flies get their name from their larvae, which exist between the top and bottom margins of a leaf, feeding on the interior tissue. Adults reproduce rapidly and are prolific.

89

Where are the pests found

Leaf miners are found in the leaves, under the surface in the tissue. These flies are common pests of ornamental plants like *Gerbera* daisies and Chrysanthemums as well as vegetable crops such as Cucumber. The presence of these plants allows a nearby population to infect cannabis.

What do they do to the plant

These little creatures are a pain to get rid of. While the maggots eat and dig squiggly lines into your leaves, the adults take small dot shaped meals from the leaves. No hole is left behind, but the plant cells are damaged. The adults lay eggs into the remaining tissue. When the eggs hatch, the larvae feed off the leaves. They look like carved scribble lines. The scribble lines get bigger as the maggots grow. They chew a hole to emerge to pupate. This occurs in the soil. Once they emerge they repeat this cycle creating a larger infestation.

Leaf miners wound the leaves and open them to infection by bacteria and fungi. Leaf damage reduces yields. When the females dig to lay eggs, plants secrete a sap that attracts ants and flies, thus inviting more infestations and problems.

How they work

Leaf miner maggots eat their way through leaves creating tunnels. Adults puncture the leaf to feed and oviposit. This damage is milder than the damage done by the maggot.

General Discussion

There are many varieties of leaf miners, but it requires an expert to distinguish between species by the characteristic appearance of their tunnels. They have

Leaf miners

evolved their unique form of attack as a means of avoiding predators and chemicals harmful to them such as THC.

Reproduction rate and life cycle: Female leaf miners implant eggs in leaves—one at a time but often in close batches. Females lay 200-300 eggs depending on species. Eggs hatch in two to six days, and larvae begin tunneling. In about a week the maggots exit the leaf to pupate for about a week. The pupa is reddish brown, about 1.5mm. The pupae develop into adults and the cycle repeats. Expect two to six generations per year outdoors, but indoors a single generation can take as little as a month, and they reproduce year-round. In warm tempurature the cycle can be as little as 15 days, or up to 25 days in cooler weather. They are rare outdoors during cold seasons.

Prevention

Outdoors, insect repellent plants such as lamb's quarter, columbine or velvet leaf can be planted near cannabis to deter the leaf miners.

Control

When it comes to control, the adults should not be the main target because most adults have already mated and laid their eggs.

Leaf miner larvae are tricky to deal with, however, as they cannot always be directly contacted with spray applications of contact-kill products, and the puparia are often resistant to the chemistry.

Biocontrol agents including the parasitic wasps *Diglyphus isaea* or *Dacnusa sibirica* are common commercial choices in farms, and naturalized populations may already be associated with leaf miner populations already present.

Remove the lower canopy of cannabis plants because these flies prefer lower leaves. You can also use trap plants such as cucumber, soy bean, peas, melons, and various Solanaceae plants.

If only a few leaves are affected, remove and discard them. Naturally occurring parasitic wasps usually help control the population.

- *Beauveria bassiana* (beneficial fungi)
- Capsaicin
- Horticultural oil
- Neem oil
- Parasitoid wasps
- Pyrethrum

Mealybugs

Photo by W. Cranshaw, CSU, Bugwood.org

MEALYBUGS AND SCALE

How common are they?

Mealybugs and scale occasionally attack cannabis.

What does the pest look like?

These pests are true bugs of the insect order Hemiptera and use their proboscis, a straw-like mouth to pierce plants and suck their juices. Mealybugs and scales are closely related to one another but take their names from their appearance. Mealybugs are named for the white, "mealy" wax that covers their bodies. On plants they look like tiny puffs of cotton, usually in crevices and joints between branches. The adult female insects beneath the wax are 0.1 to 0.2 inch (2 to 4 mm) long, with flat, oval, segmented bodies. Males are tiny flying insects that do not have the females' waxy covers.

Adult female scales produce hard shells that resemble tiny "scales" or bumps on the stems and leaves of the plants. Scales vary widely within this general model: from round to oval in shape, from white to dark brown in color and from

0.1 to 0.5 inch (3 to 15 mm) in diameter. As with mealybugs, adult male scales resemble tiny flies.

Where the pest is found?

Female mealybugs plunk themselves at the nodes. Scales are found on leaf surfaces (especially the undersides), on stems and in crevices. Occasionally, scales or mealybugs colonize the stem right at the soil level, where the stem joins the roots. Mealybugs and other scale insects share several common traits. Adult males are very rarely present. Females produce hundreds of eggs over a lifetime. Once they set down, they remain in a single place for life. They exude honeydew, concentrated plant sap, just like aphids. This promotes the growth of sooty mold. Armored scales have a hard exoskeleton structure for protection that soft scales lack. Instead, soft scales and mealybugs produce copious amounts of wax for protection. This makes them somewhat resistant to the application of some sprayed treatment compounds.

What they do to the plant

Female scales and mealybugs feed on plant sap. The males, on the other hand, are short-lived, and as adults, they do not feed at all. They live only to mate with the females. Some species have developed a symbiotic relationship with ants similar to that of aphids. Ants protect and herd them to collect the honeydew, concentrated sugars that they exude as waste. If there are no ants to eat it, it's quickly colonized by sooty mold. Plants are weakened by the insects' leech-like action on their vital juices, and the honeydew droppings create mold infections on the stems and leaves. Scales and mealybugs are often vectors for plant diseases.

General Discussion

Mealybugs are considered a specialized scale. Both are in the same order as aphids and whiteflies, and are true bugs in the biological sense. Like all true bugs, they have specialized probing and sucking mouthparts, the proboscis that they use to drain plant juices.

Female scales and mealybugs do not move much as adults. They attach themselves to the plant and produce a protective layer to ward off predators while they suck the plant juices. Mealybugs cover themselves with a web of cottony wax that some potential predators avoid. Scales produce hard shells that armor them against their enemies.

Reproduction rate and life cycle: The overall life cycle is the same for both

Mealybugs: multiple life stages

Photo by W. Cranshaw, CSU, Bugwood.org

mealybugs and scales. The females produce 200 to 1,000 tiny eggs that they shelter either on or beneath their bodies. When the eggs hatch (in one to four weeks), the very small (less than 1 mm) nymphs spread out over the plant and begin to feed. In a few weeks they develop into either winged males or stationary, shelled females. The entire generation takes one to two months. Depending on the species, they produce one to six generations in a year.

Control

Mealybugs are relatively easy to eliminate on marijuana plants because the plant's structure does not offer easy places for them to hide and protect themselves.

Because of their slow rate of reproduction, they rarely cause a threat to the garden indoors or out.

Hand-wipe with sponge or cotton swab. Mealybugs tend to locate in plant crevices and other hard-to-get-to spots. A cotton swab moistened with isopropyl alcohol is an ideal tool for reaching them.

- Alcohol spray
- Limonene products kill mealybugs and scale on contact.
- Herbal sprays containing cinnamon, clove or other insect-repellent herbal oils are very effective exterminants. They kill both on contact and

by their evaporates, especially in the protected areas mealybugs choose as habitats.

- Pyrethrum
- Neem oil
- Parasitoid wasps that are specific to various species of mealybugs and scale are available. Some species include *Leptomastix dactylopii*, *Anagyrus pseudcocci* and *Metaphycus helvolus*.
- Mealybug destroyer: *Cryptolaemus montouzieri* is a ladybug that preys on many species of mealybugs
- The minute pirate bug (*Orius* species) eats mealybugs and scale, among other pests.
- Green Lacewing
- The lady beetle *Ryzobius lophanthae* is a voracious soft-scale predator. It is opportunistic and also eats aphids and mealybugs when it encounters them. However, it is most effective on scale.
- Horticultural oil, especially sesame oil products.
- Insecticidal soaps
- Sticky Tape Traps: Use early in the season to catch crawlers. Wrap tape around the base of the stem. Scale crawlers stick to it as they crawl up the plant.

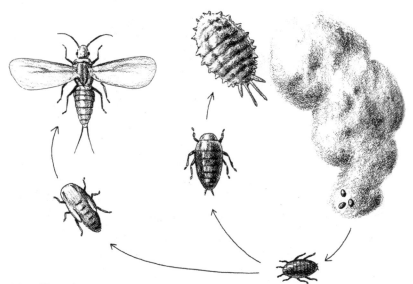

Mealybug life cycle

Spider mites congregating

MITES

The term "mite" encompasses thousands of different arthropod species, most of them well under one millimeter in length — roughly the size of the head of a pin —and the largest mite common to cannabis is roughly half that size.

Three types of mite account for almost all infestations of cannabis: Broad mites, Hemp Russet Mites and Two-Spotted Spider Mites. They range from difficult to impossible to spot without magnification and reproduce rapidly. This means, with the smaller species particularly, the damage is what you see first and by then there are already multiple generations of mites inhabiting and destroying your plant. It's more or less impossible to control a full-blown mite population bloom, so it's especially crucial to maintain preventative conditions and regularly inspect plants so action can be taken as early as possible if mites do appear.

When it comes to greenhouse grows the primary source of mites is infected clones, so in addition to proper sanitation, great care must be taken when sourcing new genetics. Biocontrol of a mite infestation needs to be established before flowering, otherwise the reduced light times will cause a clustering response in the mites, rendering predatory mites all but useless. If mites are detected early enough, before too much damage has been done to the affected plants, their numbers can be effectively thinned by spraying plants with water, but additional control methods are required to fully eliminate them.

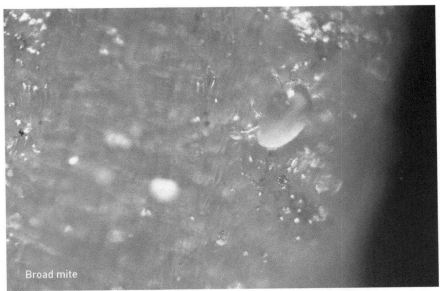

Broad mite

Photo by W. Cranshaw, CSU, Bugwood.org

BROAD MITES Actual size 0.1-0.2mm

How common are they?

The broad mite or, *Polyphagotarsonemus Latus*, is a new pest in cannabis gardens and sightings are becoming more common.

What does the pest look like?

The most notable thing about the broad mite's appearance is its diminutive size. They are so small that a 60x loop or stronger is recommended to properly identify them. With the naked eye you will only notice a large infestation, clusters of egg sites and the telltale broad mite damage. Up close the broad mite has a structure and appearance similar to larger mite species. Its coloration can vary, but often it looks like a pale yellow or clear dewdrop with tiny legs. Broad mites have a large cephelathorax, two pairs of small front legs, one pair in the middle of its body, and a wispy pair of back legs; which are more pronounced in the smaller males. Under a microscope they have a medium-size head with a definitive mandible structure. Broad mite eggs are translucent, round and with white spots. These are actually tuffs of spine-like hair, but appear as spots. They are 0.08mm in diameter.

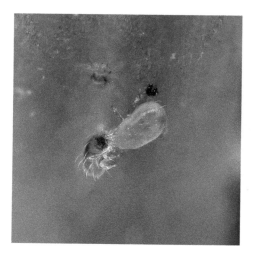

To target Spider Mites, Clover Mites, Broad Mites and Cyclamen Mites, Neoseiulus Californicus from Biotactics, is a hearty and effective Type II predator that will lay one egg for every 4-6 units of food (spider mite adult/ nymph/ egg). Effective on almost every plant from roses to strawberries to cannabis and alfalfa.

Where is the pest found?

Broad mites lay eggs on the undersides of leaves. They prefer newer growth and the crevices of the cannabis plants. Always inspect the damaged growth areas with magnification, paying close attention to the ribbing of the veins on the underside of the leaves.

What does it do to the plant?

Broad mites cause two types of damage that are great clues for identifying them. The first is often "stipling," which is a pattern of yellow dots on the leaves. These are the tiny feeding sites from the infestation. Often stipling is inconspicuous, but the leaves turn darker. As time passes after the initial wounding the sites become yellow to gray or even necrotic. These yellow speckled leaves as well as a twisting and/or yellowing of new growth are the second signs of damage. This is a result of the mites feeding. If you see these two signs in a garden, use a 60x loop to look for broad mites.

General discussion

Mites are vectors for infections, but their main damage is the sucking out of nutrients from the plants' leaves, which interferes with photosynthesis. Draining liquids and nutrients from the leaves slows down the plants' growth. This, along with vectors they can carry, and excrement and secretions lead to telltale damage in new growth.

Prevention

Prevention of broad mites can be tricky. It's difficult to surmise where they came from in many instances. Often they come in the wind, infected plant material, or are deposited by animals. One of the most likely sources of infection is importing infected clones. For this reason, many growers start plants only from seed. A good integrated pest management program is always recommended. A periodic spray with an herbal pesticide is a good start.

Controls

- Citric acid
- Herbal oils:
- Cinnamon
- Clove
- Peppermint
- Rosemary
- Thyme

A product called Nuke Em produced by flying skull is effective at eradicating broad mites. It contains potassium sorbate and yeasts.

Debug, a product described in aphid treatment and control, can be used to combat broad mites. Neem oil can be effective, but this concentrated formulation is much more effective.

Azamax and other azadirachtin-concentrated amendments are also effective and allowed in most regulated states.

Attack Spider mites, Clover Mites, Broad Mites, and Bank's Grass Mites in the vegetative state or bloom state with Neoseiulus Fallacis, a cousin of Californicus. From Biotactics, this is hearty and aggressive predatory mite and will overwinter in the soil and cover crop in hibernation and is used on tens of thousand of acres of coastal California strawberry farms and min farms in Southern Oregon.

Adult russet mite

RUSSET MITES

How common are they?

Aculops cannabicola first appeared in Serbia and Hungary in the 1960s. This cannabis specific mite is still not common but is spreading quickly through the country.

What does the pest look like?

They are smaller than conventional spider mites but larger than the broad mite so a 30x or larger magnification may be necessary to fully identify an infestation. They are built slightly differently than the spider or broad mites as well, having an elongated body, often described as carrot shaped. They have a clear to milky color makes them almost look like larvae of some other pest. Russet mites have only four legs instead of eight like other mites.

Where is the pest found?

Like the other mites, they will be located on the undersides of leaves. Russet mites work their way up plants, preferring the younger soft terminal leaves, so they are found on leaves just above damaged leaves and stems.

What do they do to the plant?

The mites suck precious sap and nutrients from the leaves and petioles of the plant. This causes a type of stippling that often turns orange or yellow "russet-ing." Soon the infected leaves die and drop off from the damage. As the colony progresses up the plant it inevitably weakens and dies.

General Discussion

All mite populations have the potential to increase numbers quickly when environmental conditions are favorable. For the three species of mites listed in this book that mostly pertains to rises in temperature. As air temperature reaches favorable conditions for cannabis growth, it also increases the mites' rates of metabolism and reproduction. A space that peaks at 85°F decreases the mites' time to sexual maturity as well as their gestation time. They do not multiply quickly compared to other mites.

Sometimes a clean-out and a replacement crop is better than fighting them as they multiply logarithmically.

Prevention

- Inspect clones entering the garden.
- Quarantine plants for several weeks before introducing them to the nursery. Sometimes ins mites can lay dormant for a bit or colonies can be so small they go unnoticed.
- Never take clones from plants that have been infected even if they have been treated and seem fine. This can serve to minimize the spread of

To treat Spider Mites and Russet Mites, apply Galendromus Occidentalis during the vegetative Bloom stage. This Western Predatory mite can withstand hot arid summers and can be applied with crop dusters and drones for precise application.

these very tiny and hard-to-control mites.

- Have predatory mites present. Amblyseius swirskii and Amblyseius cucumeris are two predators that will prevent high populations of russet mites.
- Maintaining a tidy garden and observing clean gardening habits won't protect you from this particular pest as it is mostly introduced. There are large concerns over the future of this now international traveler and commercial hemp crops worldwide.

Russet mite damage

Control

The russet mite works its way up plants from the bottom. So remove damaged leaves. Quarantine and treat the infected plant.

The damage mites can cause in a hot grow room can easily be so substantial during the first three weeks of flowering that starting over in a clean room with new plants maybe an economically better option. Russet mites have been reported to be particularly resistant to neem and other horticultural oils so this throw-'em-out and start-over mentality may prove doubly in order instead of a pitched chemical battle.

In hemp fields the introduction of predatory mites can prove effective. Using biological control measures outdoors can have it's issues, but if its timed right and multiple applications of predatory mites are used in intervals of four to seven days, the damage can be minimized enough to have a successful yield. Russet mites remove cell content from the leaves with piercing, sucking mouth parts.

Azadiractin

Citric acid

Herbal oils: Cinnamon, Clove, Geranium, Peppermint, Rosemary, Thyme

Potassium salts of fatty acids

Sulfur: Micronized sulfur applied as directed.

Spider mite Photo by Biotactics

SPIDER MITES Actual size: .02" • 0.5 mm

How common is it?

Spider mites are very common. They are the most serious pests in the cannabis garden.

What does the pest look like?

Spider mites are barely visible with the naked eye since they are only 0.06 inch (1.5 mm) long. They are arachnids (relatives of spiders), and like other arachnids, they have four pairs of legs and no antennae. Like spiders, they have two body segments. Their colors range from red, brown and black to yellow and green depending on the species and the time of year. Spider mites are so tiny though that most of these details are visible only with a magnifier. Spider mites make silk, hence the name spider mite.

The two-spotted spider mite, the spider mite most likely to attack cannabis gardens, has two dark spots visible on its back when it is an adult.

Where the pest is found

They live on the plants, mostly on the underside the leaves, but can be found on the buds. They can also be found moving along their silvery webbing, from leaf to leaf and even plant to plant.

What it does to the plant

Spider mites pierce the surface of the leaves and then suck the liquids from cells. These punctures appear on the leaves as tiny yellow/brown spots surrounded by yellowing leaf.

Identify infestation by tiny spots on the leaves. They can be seen as colored dots on the leaf undersides. As the population grows they produce webbing that the mites use as a protective shield from predators, a nursery for their eggs and a pedestrian bridge between branches or plants.

How they work

Spider mites pierce cells and suck their liquids. They are more of a threat than most pests because of their high rate of reproduction.

General Discussion

Spider mites are by far the most fearsome of all plant pests. They suck plant juices, weakening the plants. Spider mites multiply quickly. They are most active in warmer climates than cold ones

Reproduction rate and life cycle: Newly hatched mites are 3:1 female: male, and each female lays up to 200 eggs, 1 to 5 per day, as an adult. This life cycle can repeat as often as every eight days in warm, dry conditions such as a grow

Targeting Spotted Spider Mites and Pacific Mites, Mesoseiulus Longipes is the rarest predatory mite species in the world and is perfect for high elevation growing as well as dry desert areas, and is available from Biotactics.

1) Spider mites and mite eggs on a leaf   2) Spider mite webbing
3) Mites congregating   4) Spider mite damage   All photos by W. Cranshaw, CSU, Bugwood.org

room. Spider mites spread through human transport as well as by wind in outdoor gardens.

Because of their rate of reproduction and the short time from egg to sexual maturity, a spider mite population can explode with shocking speed.

Prevention

Almost all spider mite infestations enter the garden on an infested plant, through the ventilation system or by gardeners who carry the hitchhikers into the garden. Use a fine dust filter (at least 300 microns) in the ventilation system, and never enter the grow space wearing clothing that has recently been outdoors, especially

Use Persimilis, the first predatory mite ever used as a pest management product, to attack Two Spotted Spider Mites and Pacific Spider Mites in both Vegetative and Bloom State. These Type I predators only have one prey and can eat 35 food unites (a spider mite egg or adult) per day while laying 4-7 of their own eggs. They are extremely ravenous but need 70% relative humidity for their eggs to hatch, making them a great predator for hot spots with larger infestation problems. Find them at Biotactics.

in a garden. Best practice is to keep pets out as well.

Neem oil is often used as a preventive, but always look out for webbing and for the yellow-brown spots mites leave when feeding. Infected mother plants transmit mites on their clones, so it is especially important to watch for mites in a mother room. When you spot mite symptoms take action immediately.

Growing from seed in an indoor environment is a great start to prevention in an indoor grow space.

Don't introduce plants from other spaces or quarantine new plants for several weeks.

Control

Spider mites thrive in dry climates. Increasing humidity in the vegetative and early flowering stages can slow population increase.

- Insecticidal soap kills many of the mites, lowering the population and the damage, but does not eliminate the population.
- Pyrethrum is effective against some mite populations, but others have developed immunity to it.
- Cinnamon-clove tea
- Herbal pesticides

Predator mites: There are many varieties of predator mites. Get those best suited to the environment of the garden. Apply predator mites at the earliest sign of infestation. Most predator species reproduce faster than spider mites, but if the mites get a good head start, the predator population can never catch up. Even in optimal conditions, control with predator mites is very difficult. Four effective species are *Phytoseiulus persimilis, Amblyseius swirskii, Amblyseius fallacis* and *N. californicus.*

- Green lacewings
- Minute pirate bugs
- *Beauveria bassiana* (beneficial fungi)
- Capsaicin
- Carbon dioxide
- Cinnamon oil
- Coriander oil
- Fish oil
- Garlic
- Herbal oils
- Horticultural oil
- Insecticidal soaps
- Limonene
- Neem oil
- *Saccharopolyspora spinosa* (beneficial bacteria)
- Sesame oil

In warm indoor gardens, things can get out of hand quickly. If the infestation is noticed on a new crop, it may be more advantageous to cull that crop and clean the grow room with a light bleach solution. Additional measures include waiting 10 or more days and recleaning in case of a substantial outbreak. When treating plants, it is always advisable to remove lower leaves that contain large amounts of eggs. This along with repetitive spraying may be necessary.

Spider mite infected cola

- Several other predatory mites feed on spider mites,
- *Feltiella acarisuga*, the predatory spider mite fly
- *Stethorus punctillum.* the spider mite lady beetle

MOLES

How common are they?

Moles are common in temperate rural areas, less so in cities and suburbs. They may gravitate to outdoor cannabis fields because cultivation loosens the soil and makes it more hospitable to the insects that moles eat.

What does the pest look like?

Moles are burrowing mammals about 5 to 7 inches long, weighing 3 to 4 ounces. They have soft dark fur, very small eyes, pointed snouts and strong digging claws on their front feet. Moles seldom appear on the surface, though. The gardener usually notices their burrows instead.

Where the pest is found

Moles build tunnel complexes in rich soil. They eat insects and earthworms and therefore favor moist soils with a lot of soil-dwelling insect life.

What do they do to the plant

Moles seldom damage plants directly. However, their tunnels and mounds may allow plant roots to become dry, and their holes create a hazard for careless walkers.

General Discussion

The most important consideration in dealing with moles is distinguishing them from gophers, which are much more destructive. The marijuana farmer has little to worry about from moles, once she or he is sure they are moles. The clearest distinction between them and gophers is the shape of their diggings: a molehill tends to be a rough cone with a hole or an earthen "plug" near the center. A gopher mound is more fan-shaped, with the hole or plug near the narrow end.

Reproduction rate and life cycle: Moles generally have one litter of two to five pups per year, in mid to late spring. Except for the spring breeding period, they tend to be solitary and highly territorial. They fight other moles even to the death if one invades another's tunnel system.

Prevention

If you are planting directly in the soil, line the planting hole on the bottom and sides with hardware cloth. Repellents may work in outdoor gardens. A number of manufacturers sell devices that they claim repel moles by sending irritating vibrations through the soil. However there is some controversy over whether they work consistently. Odor repellents such as predator urine may be more effective, but the best-attested repellent is castor oil, sold in various brand-name formulations.

Control

If moles aren't causing root damage then there is really no need to get rid of them. However, if it is necessary to rid the garden of moles then the methods are the same as for gophers: fumigation or trapping. The commercial fumigant cartridges sold for gophers also work against moles, as does carbon dioxide from dry ice or a tank. Garden supply shops sell many kinds of mole traps, both the live-trap and lethal kind.

RATS

How common are they?

Rats are not common pests in marijuana gardens, but they sometimes kill plants by gnawing or digging. They are a very environment-specific problem, as they view cannabis as a target of opportunity.

What does the pest look like?

Rats are rodents ranging from 10 to 16 inches (25 to 40 cm) in length, not including their long tails. They weigh 6 to 12 ounces (170 to 340 grams) and have dark fur ranging from brown to black. Their heads are long and taper to a snout with long whiskers, and their ears are rounded and prominent.

Where the pest is found

Rats are common wherever humans live, although they are not always visible. Some rats live in the wild, feasting on insects, other small animals, nuts, fruits and nature's detritus. They lair in burrows, walls, piles of trash, dense brush, attics—wherever they can build a secure nest.

What they do to the plant

Marijuana is not a primary food source for rats. In fact, they may not eat it at all. Instead, rats like to chew the woody stalks of plants, cutting the plants down. The rats usually simply leave it at that, not eating the rest of the plant. A rat's teeth grow constantly throughout its life, and this gnawing behavior is instinctive to keep the teeth from getting too long.

General discussion

Rats do not look for marijuana plants; they go after them only if they're convenient. So rats are a problem for the marijuana garden only when the grow site is close to something that they do like to eat. Gardens are at risk for damage by rats near cornfields, orchards, food warehouses, areas with nuts or berries growing wild and similar places. Food at campsites draws rats close to the garden, so secure all food and destroy or remove all food scraps.

Reproduction and life cycle: Rats are prolific breeders that breed year-round if they have adequate food and a warm place to keep their young. Each female can produce four to nine litters a year (of which anywhere from 12 to 60 young live to adulthood). They adjust their population automatically to the local food supply.

Prevention

An ounce of prevention is worth many pounds of cure with rats. They do their damage in a matter of minutes, and a single rat can destroy several plants in one night. By the time you know you have a rat problem, it is often too late. Humans have been fighting rats for thousands of years, and if numbers are any guide, then the rats are at least holding their own.

Minimize the amount of rat tasty food in the area. Clear away brush and trash and plant as far as you can from attractions such as fruit trees or berry bushes. If you know of stray cats in the neighborhood of your garden, put out food to attract them. Rats avoid areas that smell of cats.

Aside from cats, the most effective prevention is a physical barrier to keep the rats away from the plants. Because cannabis isn't a primary food for rats, they won't try as hard to get it as they would if they actually liked to eat it.

An effective barrier needs to be at least 18 inches (45 cm) high and have no opening larger than 0.5 inch (12.5 mm). A simple way to meet these requirements is to wrap a tomato cage in chicken wire or hardware cloth and put one of these around each of the plants when you set them out. Another is to buy coarse steel wool (sold in bulk at hardware stores) and wrap it around the stalk of each plant, securing it with twist ties.

Control

Traps and poison provide protection. Hardware and garden stores carry a variety of effective rat traps. Place traps around the plant cage, using an attractive bait such as peanut butter. Once a few rats have been trapped, predators may come to enjoy the carrion, making the area unattractive to the rodents.

Rats have begun to develop resistance to warfarin, the classic anticoagulant "rat poison." Another problem with this poison is that it can kill predators that eat the dead rats. A newer poison is cholecalciferol (vitamin D_3). Another is zinc phosphide. Both are available in various brand-name rodent baits. Place any such poison bait in a tamper-proof bait station.

SLUGS AND SNAILS

How common are they?

Slugs and snails occasionally attack outdoor gardens. They are rare indoors.

What does the pest look like?

Slugs range in color from pale gray to tan and grow to as long as 2 inches (5 cm). Their bodies are soft and fleshy, and glisten with a clear slime that they secrete to retain moisture and help their movement. Two small "horns" atop the slug's head are actually the slug's eyes. These sense light; slugs have no of sight of objects.

Snails are slugs with shells. They are built almost identically to slugs, except for a coiled shell of calcium carbonate that protects most of a snail's body. A snail can withdraw completely into its shell when threatened. The shells of common garden snails can reach up to 1.5 inches (3.75 cm) in diameter, and come in various shades of gray, brown, and black, sometimes with markings, depending on the species.

Where the pest is found

Slugs and snails are found on the leaves and edges of leaves and flowers. During the day they rest in moist cool areas such as under debris or wood.

What they do to the plant

They eat leaves. Holes in leaves and/or clipped edges of leaves and flowers, accompanied by a silvery, slimy trail, indicate snail or slug damage. A single snail can savage several small plants in one night.

Banana slug

General discussion

They thrive in moist, dark environments. They hide in mulch, in short and stubby plants, under boards, and in soil, and they avoid sunlight, so they are seldom seen during the day but come out to feast at night.

There is one particular kind of snail that you should leave alone. So-called decollate snails sometimes attack plants, but their main food is other snails and slugs. The fastest way to tell a "good" snail from a plant-eating pest is the shape of the shell: common garden snails usually have round shells that coil in a simple spiral. Most species of decollate snails have cone-shaped shells. If these are the only snails you ever see in your garden, then go ahead and get rid of them, because they eat plants if there is no other food in their habitat. But if you have other snails as well, then the decollate snail is your friend.

Reproduction rate and life cycle: Slugs and snails are hermaphroditic and can fertilize themselves if no mate is available. They lay clutches of 30 to 120 eggs 1 to 2 inches (2.5-5 cm) deep in moist soil. When conditions are suitable (not too dry or too cold), slugs and snails can lay eggs as often as once a month, so their numbers can increase rapidly during damp spring and fall weather.

Prevention and control

The best way to prevent and kill snails and slugs is with iron phosphate, some-times called ferric phosphate. It is completely effective and requires little effort. It comes as a powder or granules and is not harmful to plants, pets or humans. Sprinkle on the ground as directed. Many brands are available.

Diatomaceous earth sprinkled around the base of the stems helps keep out slugs and snails, but it can also hinder beneficial insects.

A number of methods can be used to prevent snail or slug damage. Reduce damage dramatically by watering in the morning instead of the evening. The soil has time to dry out and become less attractive to the pests.

Place copper wire, tape or mesh around the garden or at the base of the plants. Copper shocks the pests and deters them (dimes and quarters work as well). When enclosing the garden or plants with copper, make sure not to trap the snails inside.

Slugs love beer! Bury a container of beer in the garden, leaving it just barely above the ground so they can drink it and drown. Salt causes their bodies to shrivel up.

Predators including firefly larva, toads, frogs, fireflies, snakes, birds and black iridescent beetles like snails. Firefly larvae eat slugs and snails viciously. Snails and slugs can be trapped. Construct a cool moist area for them to retreat to during the heat of the day.

Made from food grade essential oils, Ed Rosenthal's Zero Tolerance Omri pesticide attacks all soft-bodied insects, repeals infections before they even start and will leave you with products that test clean, since it completely dissolves and leaves no residue.

Thrip infestation   Photo by W. Cranshaw, CSU, Bugwood.org

THRIPS Actual size: 1/15" • 1.5 mm

How common are they?

Thrips are not commonly considered pests of marijuana outdoors. However, in greenhouses they can be serious pests.

What does the pest look like?

Thrips are tiny, no more than 0.06 inch (1.5 mm) long, but can still be seen by the naked eye, often compare to a grain of rice. Adults have wings but do not fly well; they jump or fall when startled. The head and body range from yellow to dark brown and even black and white stripes. The larvae are about half the size of adults, lighter in color, and wingless. One of the most common species on cannabis is the onion thrips, (thrips tabaci). Another common species is the western flower thrips (Frankliniella occcidentalis).

Where the pest is found

Thrips attack the leaves and are usually found on the top surface of the leaf.

What it does to the plant

Thrips use a saw-like structure to pierce and scrape the flesh until sap begins to flow. They then suck up the juices and leave a surface of patchy white or silvery scrapes. The leaf surface looks scarred or scabby. Eventually, the leaves look like all the chlorophyll has been drained, and they turn white. Thrips leave behind greenish black specks of poop on and under leaves. Thrip damage can resemble that of spider mites or leaf miners at first, but more severe cases result in the color-stripped leaves.

Damaged leaves can't be healed and their ability to absorb light is compromised. If thrips are not controlled, the plants die. Thrips also carry pathogens including botrytis and yellow dwarf virus that they transfer from plant to plant.

How it works

Thrips pierce the leaves, then suck out its contents. Thrips lay eggs on the plants. The larvae hatch and feed for several days before dropping down to the soil to pupate.

General discussion

Outdoors, thrips hibernate over the winter in soil and plant debris. They become active when the temperature climbs above 60°F (16°C). The warm, stable temperatures of indoor gardens allow them to be active year-round. Thrips are a more serious problem indoors because of this, and also because a natural soil-dwelling fungus that infects thrips pupae is not present indoors.

Reproduction rate and life cycle: Females lay eggs (anywhere from 40 to 300 depending on species) in plant crevices or actually insert them into the leaves and stems. The larvae feed until they enter the pupal stage, when they fall to the ground, where the soil fungi provide some biocontrol outdoors. Depending on the species and temperature (optimum is 77 to 82°F [26 to 28°C], the larval thrips hatch, pupate and mature to egg-laying adults in 7 to 30 days.

Out of the 5,000+ thrips species that have been documented, there are only a select few that are problematic, mainly the western flower thrips (*Frankliniella occidentalis*), which attacks many plants species. Thrips damage is unique: preferring to live on the underside of the leaf where they feed, small white or silvery dotting can be observed on the top side. Thrips themselves have a very specific body, often referred to as "cigar-shaped"; larvae have a long abdomen that tapers to a point, and are often cream-colored. Adults have feathery wings and though they have a similar body, are larger than the larvae.

Clockwise from top left: 1) Thrips congregating 2) Single thrip
3) A thrip curtain at Harborside Farms 4) Thrip damage
Photos 1-3 by W. Cranshaw, CSU, Bugwood.org. Photo 4 by Ed Rosenthal

Western flower thrips populations have become resistant to many pesticides.

Several biological control organisms have been used effectively in other crops for population control, such as various predatory mites, as well as the minute pirate bug (*Orius insidiousis*) and predatory mites A. swirskii and A. cucumeris.

Prevention

Thrips are drawn to the colors blue and yellow, so it's best to avoid having yellow walls or items around your cannabis gardens. Yellow and blue sticky cards can be used as indicator traps to detect an infestation of thrips. Use garlic in outdoor gardens to deter/repel thrips.

BioCeres WP spores adhere to the insect's body, germinating then penetrating the cuticle and growing inside, causing white muscardine disease. It will kill insects within 72 hours of application. Targets thrips, whiteflies and aphids. OMRI Listed for organic production. Perfect tank mix partner with AzaGuard.

Control

- Barrier: Thrips pupae live in the soil after they drop from the plant. By placing a cover around the top of the container, the pupae can't get to the soil and they die. As with fungus gnat larvae, a layer of *dry* diatomaceous earth on top of the soil prevents the thrips pupae from getting to the moist soil.
- *Beauveria bassiana* (beneficial fungi)
- Beneficial nematodes: If there are beneficial nematodes present they attack the pupae in the soil.
- Capsaicin
- Cinnamon oil
- Clove oil
- Coriander oil
- Horticultural oil
- Insecticidal soaps
- Minute pirate bugs (*Orius*): These insects are tiny, but they attack adult thrips. They work well with nematodes. Steinernema feltiae
- Neem oil
- Predatory mites *Amblyseius Neoseiulus*
- Pyrethrum

VOLES

How common are they?

Voles are common in temperate areas, especially those adjacent to large fields or wooded areas. Unlike their relative, the house mouse, they prefer the outdoors and staying low.

What does the pest look like?

The vole is a small rodent that has a brownish to grayish coloration with small ears, eyes and tail. The vole has seven toes on his front paws and five toes his rear.

Where is the pest found?

A great indicator of a vole problem is the presence of the trails they build as they go to and fro. Droppings and nests with a litter of young are frequently found along their routes.

What they do to the plant

Voles can wreak havoc on young plants by gnawing the stalk near the base. They also can tunnel through root systems, causing plants to die back or lean over.

General discussion

Voles are known as meadow mice or field mice in North America. There are approximately 155 species of voles. They are small rodents measuring from 3 to 9 inches in average length. They are mostly known for girdling or eating around the base of plants but may also attack root systems.

Prevention

Voles like to hide in low vegetation or garden refuse so keep a clean garden floor free from weeds and waste. Remove places where they can hide such as piles of garden supplies or wood piles.

Controls

A cat in the garden deters voles.

Predator urine is an effective deterrent.

Place live traps perpendicular to the most trafficked routes or near nesting sites.

Mouse traps baited with peanut butter work as well.

Encircling plant stems with light-colored tree guards or wire mesh helps save large plants from damage.

Whiteflies

WHITEFLIES 1/16" • 1.5 mm

How common are they?

Whiteflies are a common pest indoors and outdoors.

What does the pest look like?

Whiteflies resemble tiny white moths but are neither moths nor true flies. They are true bugs, relatives of aphids and scales. They are 0.04 inch (1 mm) long and their soft bodies are covered in a powdery wax which gives them protection and their white color. Whiteflies share similar traits with aphids and mealybugs. They all feed on plant sap and produce honeydew (the substrate necessary for sooty mold). Whiteflies differ from scale bugs regarding mobility. The females of scale bugs are stationary. However, only non-adult stages of whiteflies stay virtually anchored to a single place. The adults fly. Wax production is minimized in comparison to aphids and scale insects only existing either on their bodies or around eggs, which are sometimes arranged in a circular pattern. Whitefly larvea are small insects that look like green or yellow scales adhered to a leaf or stem, and are white-winged as adults, usually preferring the undersides of leaves. Large populations can severely stunt growth and grow to hundreds if given enough time.

Where the pest is found

Whiteflies infest the undersides of leaves. If the plant is disturbed, they take wing and a mass of tiny white flies can be seen fluttering around the plant.

What they do to the plant

They suck sap from the plants and are vectors for broad mites and powdery mildew. The plants release sticky honeydew, which can contribute to mold problems on the plants. Leaves appear spotty, droop and lose vigor.

How they work

Whiteflies are sap-feeders, like their relatives, aphids and scales.

Correct pest identification is critical for a successful IPM program. ARBICO's Yellow Pest Insect Traps can be used to attract, trap and monitor pest insects as well as to monitor infestations and to know your pest thresholds and are waterproof for potted plants, greenhouses, or outdoors.

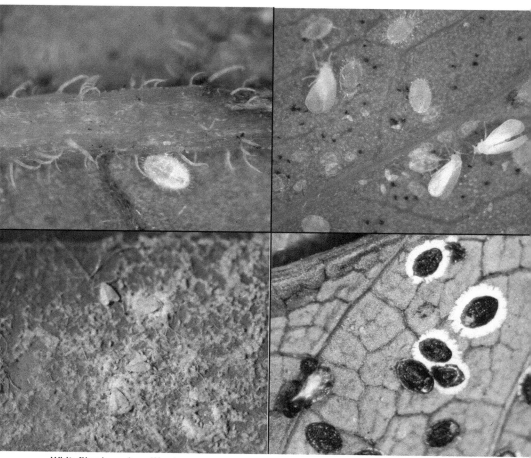

Whiteflies in various life stages

General discussion

Whiteflies are a pest in big numbers but are not difficult to get rid of. If you think the plants might have whiteflies but are unsure, shake them. You'll see them flying off, then settling right back onto the leaves.

Reproduction rate and life cycle: Females each lay about 100 tiny eggs on the undersides of leaves. Eggs hatch in about seven to ten days, and the larvae drain sap from leaves. Larvae mature in two to four weeks and the adults live for four to six weeks after that. The reproductive rate is temperature dependent: most whitefly species do best in a temperature range of 80 to 90°F (27 to 33°C).

Prevention

Keep the temperature of the garden below 80°F (27°C) to slow whitefly reproduction. Clear out plant debris quickly. Install a fine dust filter, at least 400 micron, in the air intake for the grow space to prevent whiteflies from entering through the vents.

Control

- Yellow sticky traps- Whiteflies are attracted to yellow sticky cards. These trap a small proportion of the population, but are good indicators of infestations.
- Shake plants to dislodge whiteflies and then suck them out of the air with the hose attachment of a vacuum cleaner. Heavily infested plants should be removed from the garden or grow room before treatment.
- *Encarsia formosae* are tiny wasps that lay their eggs inside immature whiteflies. They are not social; they don't make hives and are so small that once they are released you may never see them again. Indoors and in greenhouses one introduction may be all that is needed because their numbers increase much faster proportionally than their prey.
- *Beauveria bassiana* (beneficial fungi)
- Beneficial insects (lacewing larvae, minute pirate bugs)
- Capsaicin
- Carbon dioxide
- Cinnamon oil
- Cloves
- Coriander oil
- Garlic
- Herbal oils
- Horticultural oil
- Insecticidal soap
- Limonene
- Neem oil
- Parasitoid wasps
- Pyrethrum
- Sesame oil
- There are several biocontrol agents that are effective;
  Type IIIb predatory mites *Amblyseius swirskii* and *Neoseiulus cucumeris*,
  The lady beetle *Delphastus catalinae*.

Powdery mildew   Photo by Kristen Angelo

Section 3

DISEASES

D isease can strike marijuana plants at any stage. Most diseases that affect marijuana fall into two broad categories: fungal and bacterial. The spores and bacteria that cause plant diseases are ubiquitous. A garden's susceptibility to disease is often traceable to environmental imbalances in temperature, moisture, light conditions, airflow and pH, among others.

Fungus grows when it encounters the right levels of moisture, temperature (the range varies by species), acidic conditions and a reliable food source.

Bacteria are much more likely to invade when the environment has been compromised. Conditions such as oxygen deprivation make their attack more successful.

Once disease hits, it is important to act quickly to restore balance to the environment. However, prevention, by way of a balanced environment for the plants, is the best solution.

AIR FILTRATION AND SANITATION

Fungal spores often enter a grow space on air currents. A fine dust filter in the air intake system captures these spores and reduces the chance of fungal infections. Another option is a UVC lamp in the intake duct. The light from these lamps kills microbes and destroys spores. The two options can be combined.

Vital Oxide is an EPA registered disinfectant cleaner gentle enough to use without gloves. Safely eliminates mold, mildew, bacteria and viruses on both hard surfaces and fabric with no damage to treated articles. It can even be fogged into HVAC to neutralize mold spores. A powerful odor eliminator, it contains no VOC (Volatile Organic Compounds). No rinse required on food contact surfaces, just spray and walk away.

THE PROBLEMS

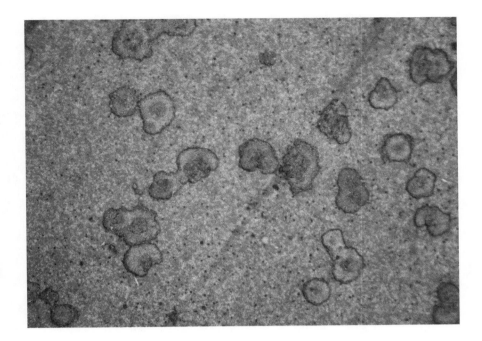

ALGAE

Algae are plantlike, usually microscopic organisms. Some are unicellular and others form multicelled organisms. They conduct photosynthesis like larger plants but lack stems, roots and leaves.

How common is it?

Algae occasionally grow in hydroponic and aeroponic systems.

Origin

Algae thrive in environments that provide warm temperature, light and nutrients. The water temperature 68-72°F (22°C), which is best for maximum plant growth, is, unfortunately, a good temperature for algae.

When light shines on nutrient-rich water, algae are almost guaranteed to grow.

Where the disease is found

Algae can grow anywhere in your system. It is commonly found inside tubes, in nutrient reservoirs, in buckets, on exposed rockwool cube surfaces and in DWC (deep water culture) buckets—mainly if the containers are not opaque and allow light in).

All containers should be opaque.

Appearance and effect of the disease

Some algae attach to surfaces such as tubes and reservoir surfaces as well as roots. They form a green film that looks and feels either velvety or slimy. When it covers the roots, it starves them of oxygen. The film also competes for nutrients and can clog system lines, motors and sprayers in aeroponic systems.

Algae photosynthesize during the day, using CO_2 dissolved in the water and releasing oxygen (O_2). However, during the dark period algae use oxygen dissolved in the water and release CO_2. This depletes the water of oxygen, which the roots require to maintain health.

Prevention

The best way to prevent algae is to deprive it of light. This is a safe, nonchemical method of prevention. Use black tubing, rather than clear or translucent, to prevent light from coming into the lines. Use a black or opaque reservoir to hold the water/nutrient solution. Make sure the cover is opaque and light-tight. Potting containers should be opaque.

Everything should be light-proof. Rock-wool cubes should also be covered. You can use landscape sun-block fabric, white-black plastic (white side up) or plastic rock-wool cube covers made for the purpose.

Control

The best method of algae control is by excluding light. This should be the main emphasis in systems with algae problems. If you already have algae growing, clean the system and replace or cover light- transmitting tubing and reservoirs with opaque materials. Panda plastic (white-black flexible polyethylene plastic) can be used to cover systems to ensure opacity. It can be used indoors or outdoors.

If algae are still a problem, rest assured that there is a light leak in the system. Algae need light.

Green algae

Other methods of controlling algae:

- H_2O_2—A 0.5-1% hydrogen peroxide solution stops algae and other organisms but must be used regularly. It should not be used with mycorrhizae because H_2O_2 kills both good and bad microorganisms.
- **Colloidal silver**—A solution of a few parts per million (ppm) colloidal silver prevents algae growth and, like H_2O_2, kills all microorganisms.
- **UVC light**—This is considered a germicidal light and is often used to keep hot tubs, fish tanks and other water free from microorganisms.
- **Grapefruit seed extract**—Grapefruit seed extract kills algae without harming plants. This method is used by water supply systems for keeping drinking water, ponds and lakes algae-free.

Top and right photo by Fred Morledge

GRAY MOLD AND BROWN MOLD (BOTRYTIS)

Gray mold, *Botrytis cinerea*, is found almost everywhere and can cause disease on most plants, including marijuana. It can cause damping off and stem canker but is most serious when it causes bud rot.

How common is it?

Gray mold is one of the most common fungal diseases that attack marijuana.

Origin

Although gray mold can infect seeds pre-germination, it is much more commonly encountered causing moldy growth of the flowers and foliage much later in development.

The fungus can germinate only on wet plant tissue when the temperature is between 55-70°F (13-21°C). This often happens in dry weather as dew accumulates on the leaves. Once it starts growing, it can tolerate a wide range of humidity and temperatures, but high humidity and cool temperatures help it thrive. Lowering the humidity stops its continued growth.

Gray mold, like most other fungi, enters and easily infects any part of a plant that is wounded, damaged from pests and pruning or beginning to die. Thus it is very important to sanitize pruning equipment between cuts.

Cuts and lesions are a normal part of plant life, so all plants are subject to attack when conditions are favorable to the mold. Unhealthy or shaded areas of plants or crevices in buds are ideal conditions for the mold. Spores travel mostly via wind and rain and even in tap water, but they can be brought into grow rooms on clothing and pets.

Where the disease is found

Shaded areas of the plant that do not get a lot of light are usually first infected. Then the disease spreads quickly through growth and spores.

Gray mold does the greatest amount of damage during flowering. It attacks the flowering tops, leaves and stalks. Seedlings and seeds can also be infected and killed.

Eliminator is an OMRI-listed, revolutionary green solution that kills and eliminates molds, mildews and soft-bodied insects on your indoor and outdoor gardens. Apply from start to finish, this oil free insecticide and fungicide will also increase at your yield.

Appearance and effect of the disease

Gray mold starts out whitish like powdery mildew but then darkens to a smoky gray or brown color. It has a fuzzy appearance and light to dark brown rot forms in the damaged tissue.

Leaves and buds break down from being suffocated by the mold. In higher humidity, the gray-yellow mold leaves a brown slimy substance on the leaves and turns the bud to rot, especially when the tissue is dense late in flowering. When the mold dries, it leaves dark brown areas of infection. Dense buds are most susceptible because the moisture is trapped in the crevices. Sometimes only part of the bud is infected.

Stems with unhealed breaks can be infected with *B. cinerea* causing stem cankers, which then affect the rest of the plant by depriving it of nutrients and water.

Prevention

Indoors, avoid conditions favorable to gray mold by controlling humidity and temperature. Keep humidity under 50%. Water when your grow lights are on or during the day. Remove and discard dead or dying plant tissue. Make sure no moisture is on leaves and buds when the lights go out. Gray mold indoors is usually caused by high humidity.

To eliminate powdery mildew, mold, fungus, spider mites and soft body insects, without using poison, use Lost Coast Plant Therapy that leaves no residue and is safe to use up to the day of harvest.

Mold

Outdoors, you can't control the weather but you can prevent bud rot. *Bacillus subtilis* is a bacterium that attacks B. cinerea. It can be sprayed on the plant as a preventive.

Potassium bicarbonate ($KHCO_3$) and pH Up change the pH of the environment from acidic to alkaline. Alkaline environments inhibit the germination of molds and fungi, including gray mold.

Sulfur is often used as a spray or vapor to control fungi.

Neem oil and sesame oil form a barrier and inhibit mold germination.

Control

If you see gray mold or stem wounds, apply a fungicide. The mold is particularly difficult to remove from plants in late flowering.

Removing the mold from living bud to prevent its spread may do more harm than good unless done carefully. The very act of fiddling with them may help transfer the mold to new sites. Sterilize tools by dipping them in alcohol or hydrogen peroxide after curing a bud.

- *Bacillus pumilus* (beneficial bacteria)
- Clove oil
- Compost and compost tea
- Copper
- Coriander oil
- Neem oil
- Potassium bicarbonate
- *Pseudomonas* (beneficial bacteria)
- Quaternary amines
- Sesame and fish oil
- Sodium bicarbonate
- Sulfur: spray, vaporizer or burner
- *Trichoderma* (beneficial fungi)

LEAF SEPTORIA

Leaf Septoria, or yellow leaf spot infection is one of the most common types of leaf spot diseases, but it mostly affects outdoor plants. It is primarily spread by "wind, water and walking," so in those rare instances that an indoor grow is affected it's generally because spores blew in from a very near outside source or were carried inside by shoes worn on infected soil. The disease isn't usually fatal to infected cannabis plants but it does radically reduce yields because of its disruption of leaf photosynthesis.

Origin

Two closely related fungi, *Septoria cannabis* and *S. neocannabina*, cause yellow leaf spot. Yellow leaf spot is a wet and cloudy warm weather infection. Warm water and rain trigger the release of spores from the storage structures so it usually appears mid to late season. Infections occur when the temperature is in the 60's, but the fungi grow faster and are more destructive as the temperature rises, with its ideal temperature just below 80° F (25° C).

Where the disease is found?

Septoria Conidia spend winter in a dormant state on residual plant material in the topsoil. Infection generally presents in early spring on juvenile plants and seedlings as spots on the upper side of the lower leaves, but has also been observed on stems and top fan leaves. It takes roughly a week for symptoms to appear after inoculation. While the infection cycle begins in spring, summer is when the disease spreads aggressively; if left unchecked, the wet, relatively warm rains will spread the conidia rapidly.

Appearance and effect of the disease

Spots begin as small round discolorations but usually expand into oblong, angular shapes, sometimes with a distinct reddish-brown border. These spots eventually desiccate and flake away from the plant, leaving jagged voids in the leaf. In extreme cases the entire leaf may curl up and wither away. The leaf damage caused by septoria infection undermines photosynthesis, which stunts growth and reduces yields of flowers, fiber and seeds.

There are other "leaf spot" infections that affect cannabis but they are relatively easy to distinguish by their presentation on the plant and obviously different when viewed under magnification. If the spots are lighter in color and do not dry up and leave holes, then it is more likely to be White Leaf Spot. Alternately, if the spots are darker and remain relatively small this may indicate a Brown Leaf Spot infection, while spots mostly presenting on the bottom of the leaf might suggest Olive Spot. Any lingering doubt can be easily erased with a glance through a microscope.

Prevention

Indoors

Plants are not likely to come in contact with the spores unless they are trekked in or there are infected outdoor plants nearby.

Outdoors

Septoria fungi are specific but ubiquitous. Only two species attack Cannabis. As a result, plants are more likely to be infected if there is marijuana, or perhaps hops, growing outdoors near the garden.

The spores overwinter on fallen infected marijuana leaves and debris and spread in three ways: wind, water and walking, either by humans and animals.

Infections are most likely to occur in gardens and spaces where marijuana has been grown before. To lessen the likelihood of infection remove all residue from the previous garden and then spray the area with a fungicide. Clean and decontaminate all tools after working with infected plants. If possible plant the garden in a different space each year.

As with all fungal plant diseases the cornerstone of prevention is proper sanitation after harvest: All residual plant matter (stalks, roots, etc.) should be shredded to uncover any pathogens or pests hiding inside, then burned, buried or composted at a separate location. All tools and materials used (and all clothing worn) during cultivation should be disinfected and/or sterilized. In a greenhouse setting, all surfaces should be thoroughly cleaned and sterilized. If possible, move the location of your grow each season.

Control

Pruning is the key to controlling septoria. When possible remove infected limbs and treat all wounds with fungicide to prevent further spread. If necessary, you can remove whole diseased plants from otherwise uninfected fields: Quickly pull a trash bag over the infected plant and cinch it at the base of the stalk before removing it from the soil to minimize the chance of spreading the infection.

- *Bacillus pumilis* (beneficial bacteria)
- Cinnamon and clove oils
- Compost and compost tea
- Neem oil
- pH Up
- Potassium bicarbonate
- Sesame and fish oils
- Sodium bicarbonate
- *Trichoderma* (beneficial fungi)

Powdery mildew   Photo by Kristen Angelo

POWDERY MILDEW

Powdery mildew is a common disease caused by several species of fungi known to infect cannabis that share hosts with many other plants (*Golovinomyces cichoracearum*, for example). Spores are ubiquitous and can travel extremely far distances on air currents, and infection is essentially invisible until the organism establishes, producing spores and a white mass that lowers the rate of photosynthesis. Powdery mildew can very quickly re-colonize the same plant or a nearby host that is suitable, making prevention an important aspect of management. Higher humidity brought on by moisture can facilitate development, but high amounts of standing water on foliage can have the opposite effect. The races that attack hops also attack marijuana.

How common is it?

Mildew spores are found everywhere. Powdery mildew is a common problem for both indoor and outdoor growers whenever the temperature and humidity fall into its favored range.

Origin

Mildew spores are ubiquitous and endemic. In areas where marijuana or hops is being grown, wind and air ventilation are the main vectors. Another major factor is contaminated cuttings. However, clothing, pets and outdoor animals can also deliver spores to the garden.

Spores can remain dormant until environmental factors, which include a suitable host, adequate humidity, moderate temperatures, low light intensity and acidity, trigger them.

Where the disease is found

Powdery mildew is most likely to attack young leaves, up to two or three weeks old. The infection spreads over the plant and to other plants in the garden. It affects buds, stems, stalks and leaves.

Appearance and effect of the disease

The first signs of an infection are raised humps on the upper leaf surfaces. Plant leaves look like they've been dusted with flour or confectionary sugar. At first it might appear on just a small portion of the leaf in an irregular circle pattern. It quickly spreads and soon the entire leaf is covered as if it had been powdered.

Infected plants prematurely yellow, brown and eventually die. If untreated, black specks can arise in the white powdery mildew. Buds have a stale, moist smell and are coated with a white powdery-looking mildew substance that can't be removed. Powdery mildew hinders photosynthesis, causing your harvest to cripple to little or no yield.

Infected cannabis buds and leaves are not acceptable for smoking.

Deliver Missing Wavelengths™ of Safe Light called Light Energy BRe³ that will give positive light energy to plants as well as negative light energy to pathogens with the BRe³ WAND to drive plant growth by accelerating the rate of photosynthesis and more ATP production to improve cell repair, plant hormone functionality, as well as naturally controlling powdery mildew, fungi and bacteria.

Prevention

Quarantine all new plants in a separate area where they can't infect other plants.

Filter incoming air to prevent spores from entering the room in the airstream.

A germicidal UVC light like the ones used in food handling kills powdery mildew spores that are airborne.

Ionizers and ozone generators precipitate and inactivate spores, lessening the chances of infection.

As with other fungi, restrict humidity and spore production by not watering or foliar spraying at night or with lights off.

Powdery mildew

Water plants when lights first come on or with at least five hours of remaining light time.

Keep humidity in check; anything over 50% may trigger problems.

To minimize plant-to-plant infection, keep plants spaced apart to allow for maximum airflow in between plants.

To prevent outbreaks, you can use the following Ampelomyces quisqualis (beneficial fungi) products on a regular basis:

- *Bacillus pumilis* (beneficial bacteria)
- *Bacillus subtilis* (beneficial bacteria)
- Compost and compost tea
- Milk
- Neem oil
- Potassium bicarbonate
- Sesame and fish oils
- Sodium bicarbonate

Control

Powdery mildew in vegetative growth is easier to treat than in the later stages of flowering. If your plants get infected during flowering, especially far into the flowering stage, the buds will eventually become infected.

Removing infected leaves from the grow room is critical. Carefully remove them without knocking spores into the air. Place a bag over infected leaves and

For a broad spectrum bactericide / fungicide that kills plant pathogens and propagules, including spores, OMRI listed ZerolTol 2.0 will protect your crop and leave no residue while preventing powdery mildew, Botrytis, and Pythium.

tie it shut; then remove the leaves. Use a fungicide on wounded stems from which you've removed the leaves.

The following products will work for indoor and outdoor plants:

- *Bacillus pumilis* (beneficial bacteria)
- *Bacillus subtilis* (beneficial bacteria)
- Cinnamon oil and tea
- Clove oil
- Copper
- Coriander oil
- Garlic
- Horticultural oils containing jojoba or cottonseed oil
- Hydrogen peroxide
- Limonene
- Milk
- Neem oil
- pH Up
- Potassium bicarbonate
- Sesame oil
- Sodium bicarbonate
- Sulfur
- Vinegar

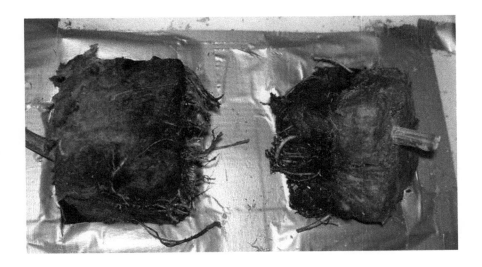

ROOT DISEASES

Every plant must have a healthy root system. Pathogens can attack and damage the roots of one plant, then rapidly infect other plants in the garden. Fusarium, Verticillium and Pythium are common and destructive root aggressors known to all growers, whether soil gardeners or hydroponicists.

Eliminate powdery mildew and other fungus with Ed Rosenthal's Zero Tolerance Fungicide. Made with essential oils that you can use up to a week before harvest to protect your plants from infection.

Fusarium

FUSARIUM

Fusarium is a complex of many different fungal species (two common species are *Fusarium oxysporum* and *F. solani*), which are able to reside in the soil for long periods. One of the more common species encountered is a pathovar, or special strain, that affects cannabis in particular (*Fusarium oxysporum* f. sp. cannabis). This strain was discovered several decades ago and was eventually considered inappropriate as a biocontrol for illegal Cannabis crops. Fusarium root rot is a common disease of many plants. It often quickly damages roots before symptoms are obvious and control can be administered effectively.

Different Fusarium species produce somewhat different diseases in cannabis. These diseases, primarily Fusarium wilt and Fusarium root rot, present different symptoms but respond to similar prevention and control methods.

How common is it?

Fusarium is not commonly found in marijuana gardens. However, residual spores are more common in soil where hemp was once grown or where it still grows as a weed. Growers using hydroponic systems or sterile or pasteurized planting mix seldom see it. Fusarium infections are most common in warm weather, but overall the frequency varies. Because Fusarium is soil-based and species-specific, it may be extremely common in one area but rare in another where the soil is not infected.

Origin

Fusarium spores can remain dormant in soil for years, and infected soil is nearly impossible to disinfect. The fungus can also spread from seed taken from infected plants.

Where the disease is found

Damage from Fusarium wilt is most evident on the leaves and stems. Fusarium root rot affects the roots first, then the disease works its way up the stem.

Appearance and effect of the disease

Fusarium wilt initially appears as small, dark irregular spots on lower leaves, which quickly become chlorotic (yellow-brown). Leaf tips curl upward, and wilted leaves dry and hang on plants without falling off. Stems turn yellow, then brown, and finally collapse. Roots show no outward symptoms if the diseased plant is pulled up.

Fusarium root rot begins below the soil line, turning the roots rotten and necrotic and giving them a characteristic red color. The first visible symptom

Designed for cannabis growers, Dynamyc™ is a mycorrhizal inoculant that is made of several strains of endomycorrhizal fungi that will create an underground web that breaks down nutrients and mobilizes them to plant roots improving plant health, yield, and cannabinoid content. The plant on the left is treated with Dynamyc™; the plant on the right is untreated.

Fusarium

usually appears as the rot works its way up the stem, producing a red-brown discoloration at the soil line. This discoloration may progress to swelling and the stem may split open. The plant soon begins to wilt, then collapses as the decay spreads up the stalk.

In both wilt and root rot, the fungus spreads through plant cells and clogs the xylem vessels, inhibiting water and nutrient transport. This vascular clogging inside the plants causes the external symptoms of wilt and collapse. Infected plants usually die. Fusarium survives in the plant debris, so infected plant debris should not be buried, composted or placed on uninfected soil.

To activate, revive and stimulate indoor hydroponic plants, outdoor plants, seedlings and more, try Reiziger Root Booster. It is nutrient-rich and will revive or help newly potted plants or transplants to grow early white roots.

Prevention

If an outdoor cannabis crop falls prey to Fusarium, that patch of ground can no longer be used to grow cannabis at all, although other plants will do fine there. Likewise, seeds produced by infected plants should not be used. The pathogen stays dormant on the seed and attacks the plant when the seedling emerges, causing damping off and likely killing it.

Avoid planting marijuana in the same ground for many years in a row. Even though none of the plants show symptoms, multiple successive plantings can cause the fungus to build up in the soil until it reaches destructive levels.

Certain soil types have been found to be less conducive to the growth of Fusarium than others. Clay soils have fungistatic properties due to their high pH. Loamy soils with healthy and diverse plant growth often harbor native microbes that suppress Fusarium. These soils do not stop the fungus, but they slow it down and may be helpful in combination with other preventive measures.

Properly aged compost, and tea made from compost, help protect plants from all sorts of fungal infections.

Container gardening is one of the best ways to avoid Fusarium, because it gives the gardener complete control over the soil. If an area that would otherwise be ideal (weather, sun, etc.) is known to be infected with Fusarium, then containers allow you to take advantage of the site's strong points while avoiding the disease issues. To prevent Fusarium infections, use sterilized or pasteurized soil mixes and new pots, and do not overfertilize. Make sure the soil drains.

Mycorrhizae (beneficial fungi) help improve plants' disease resistance.

Streptomyces griseoviridis, *Bacillus pumilus* and *Bacillus subtilis* (all beneficial bacteria) or *Gliocladium* (beneficial fungus) can be applied as pretreatments for seeds, as a soil drench or as a foliar spray.

Make sure the soil pH doesn't get too low. Neutralize acidic soil with dolomite lime or greensand. Fertilizers enhanced with potassium and calcium can help fight off and prevent Fusarium, while excess nitrogen and phosphorous may make the disease worse.

Control

The only truly effective control is the removal and destruction of infected plants. After removing any affected plants, use hydrogen peroxide (H_2O_2) to clean all the tools that touched those plants before using them again.

VERTICILLIUM WILT

How common is it?

Verticillium wilt is caused by soil-borne fungi that are common in many soils, and it attacks hundreds of herbaceous and woody plant species, including cannabis.

Origin

Verticillium wilt is a disease caused by fungi in the Verticillium group (e.g., *Verticillium dahliae* and *Verticillium albo-atrum*), which infect the leaves and roots of over 400 plant species and cause yellowing and other discoloration by blocking the water channels in the host. Small black protrusions can sometimes be a sign of an intermediate or advanced infection, usually found on dying tissue. Infected plants can be asymptomatic for a short time before the fungi start to cause wilting, which itself is not a symptom unique to Verticillium wilt, so observe caution both when evaluating the disease and after confirming its presence for treatment. Particularly moist-growing substrates encourage many kinds of pathogenic growth, including those that cause Verticillium wilt.

Where the disease is found

Verticillium wilt starts by attacking stressed roots, then proceeds to affect the leaves as well.

Appearance and effect of the disease

The lower leaves turn yellow along the margins and between the veins before turning a gray-brown and wilting. The stem turns brown near the soil line; symptoms can resemble Fusarium wilt. Once the roots have been affected, Verticillium wilt spreads through the xylem, which exhibits a brownish discoloration. The vascular system plugs up, reducing the flow of water through the roots and causing wilting.

Stressed roots

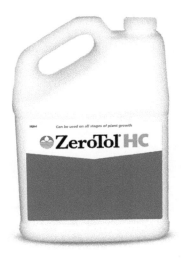

Perfect for the indoor or hydroponics grower with growing space less than 500 sq. ft. ZeroTol HC leaves no residue, and uses sustainable chemistry to keep diseases such as Powdery Mildew, Botrytis and Pythium at bay.

Prevention

Sterile planting mix and hydroponic growing systems prevent Verticillium infection. However, soil in the growing containers may carry the fungus. Many soil bacteria and fungi help to suppress Verticillium, so if sterile soil isn't an option, then amending your soil with alfalfa meal or aged compost may offer some protection. Keep the planting beds well drained, as excess moisture in the root zone greatly increases the risk of Verticillium.

Properly aged compost and compost tea help protect plants from stresses.

Control

There is no chemical control available. The best thing to do is to pasteurize the soil. A fertilizer that is low in nitrogen and high in potassium may help. Some possible biocontrols include:

- *Bacillus subtilis* (FZB24 strain)
- *Trichoderma* fungus

PYTHIUM

Pythium species belong to a phylum (formerly known as kingdom) of organisms called oomycota, which have traits similar to both fungi and other single-celled organisms that allow them to actively move to infect hosts. Another oomycota causes downy mildew. Unlike fungi, they do not build cell wall of chitin but of cellulose. Pythium infections can be present inside seed and affect seedling germination, or they can affect post-seedling emergence, one of several soil pathogens that cause the phenomenon of "damping off." Continuously moist or waterlogged substrate encourages growth and infection rates of this organism, which can quickly spread to nearby plants, especially if they share the same substrate.

Pythium is a destructive parasitic root disease. Under favorable conditions, Pythium multiplies very rapidly and releases microscopic mobile spores with tails that swim using a whiplash tail to search for roots to infect. It attacks mainly seeds and seedlings, which have little resistance to disease. Larger plants can be treated and saved if they are identified early, although your crop will be stunted.

How common is it?

Pythium is a common problem in field, container and hydroponic cultivation.

Origin

Pythium exists everywhere in the plant's environment. It is present in your growing area, no matter how clean it is. Sanitation still helps: Pythium is often described as a "secondary infection," because it attacks plants that have already been weakened by stress: disease, damage, pests, nutrient deficiencies or poor growing conditions. Providing a healthy growing environment helps to prevent infection.

The best conditions for Pythium development include high moisture levels

Great White contains 8 different species of endomycorrhizal fungi, 14 different species of beneficial bacteria and 2 species of trichoderma all in one product. Research shows that these organisms enhance plant and root development, enhances enzyme release and enhance nutrient solubility. The water-soluble powder makes application easy and delivers the spores directly to the roots for immediate germination. Users should look for enhanced root development, yields, flowering, nutrient and water absorption and transplant success.

in the soil, high humidity and a temperature between 70-85°F (20-30°C). Lack of oxygen (O) hydroponic nutrient solutions also helps Pythium take hold. An abundance of O lessens the chances of infection.

Where the disease is found

Pythium generally affects the entire plant but mainly the roots and foliage. Young plants and seedlings in both soil fields and hydroponic gardens are the most susceptible.

Appearance and effect of the disease

Look for an overall yellowing of the foliage, sometimes accompanied by browning leaf edges. The plant appears wilted or stunted. The roots become discolored, soft and watery. As the infection advances, the outer part of the roots comes off, exposing a stringy inner core. In soil gardens and containers, the roots will not be visible, but Pythium often advances from the roots to the "crown" of the plant, just above the soil line, causing the same browning and softening that it produces in the roots.

Pythium moves through soil or water to the plant roots where it germinates before entering the roots. Once in the roots, it spreads through the tissue and produces resting spores, which further germinate and can infect the roots indirectly.

Prevention

The best prevention is keeping the plants healthy and free of other pests that might give Pythium an opening. Use well-drained, pasteurized soil or soilless mixes in containers and avoid overfertilization and overwatering.

Water with high O levels helps keep the roots healthy and resist microorganism onslaughts.

Address pests, other diseases and nutrient deficiencies promptly, as these stresses make plants more susceptible to Pythium.

Properly aged compost, and tea made from compost, help protect plants from all sorts of fungal infections.

Use mychorrhizzae and trichoderma in planting mixes and rock wool. These fungi protect the roots and are antagonistic to pathogens.

Keep fungus gnats in check, as they can carry Pythium spores into containers with pasteurized soil. Note that one of the preventive measures for fungus gnats is to let the soil dry to a depth of about 1 inch (2-3 cm) between waterings, which reduces Pythium growth. A protective cover over the container or block prevents gnat larvae from borrowing in.

Prevention is especially important in hydroponic systems. Once Pythium infects these systems, it spreads through the water too quickly to stop. Keep your system as clean as possible to avoid infection.

An option for very thorough cleaning is to treat the water with hydrogen peroxide (H_2O_2) at each nutrient solution change. UVC water disinfection systems kill water-borne spores. However, these methods kill beneficial organisms in the nutrient solution as well as pathogens like Pythium. The value of this trade-off varies from one system to the next, but it is worthwhile for some growers.

Biocontrols such as those listed below are effective if applied before the plant shows any symptoms. Note that disinfection measures such as peroxide and UVC in hydroponic systems will also kill off these biocontrol agents.

- *Bacillus subtilis* (beneficial bacteria)
- *Gliocladium* (beneficial fungus)
- *Pseudomonas* (beneficial bacteria)
- *Streptomyces griseoviridis* (beneficial bacteria)

Controls

Pythium presents very similar symptoms to Phytophthora root rot in plants other than cannabis. However, while Phytophthora is a common problem in many other plants, no species is known to infect cannabis. Therefore, marijuana gardeners should verify that any control they use is listed for use against Pythium. Controls that are specific for Phytophthora are not effective.

- Clove oil
- Copper oil
- Coriander oil
- Quaternary amines
- Sesame oil
- Trichoderma (beneficial fungi)

The first hydroponic grow booster for craftsmen, Reiziger Grow Booster is tailored for short cultures. Transform plants and quickly increase biomass while amplifying aromatic compounds in a short time, this high concentration of botanical ingredients will empower the plant with energy and fortify it's natural defences while elevating aromatic terpenes, color, and resin production.

STEM ROTS—DAMPING OFF

Damping off is a condition rather than a specific disease: the rotting of seedlings underground, at the soil line or at the crown. It is caused by several seed- and soil-borne fungi, especially Rhizoctonia and Pythium. Damping off mainly affects soil growers and generally kills any seedling it affects.

How common is it?

Damping off is a common problem. It is often blamed on bad seeds, as it may destroy the seedlings even before they emerge from the growing medium.

Origin

Damping off occurs in warm, nitrogen-rich soil that stays wet for long periods. Even hydroponic systems can get damping off when the growing media become too saturated and the roots do not have a plentiful supply of oxygen. Oxygenating the water helps prevent infection.

Where the disease is found

The infection begins below the soil line and affects seedlings with up to eight sets of true leaves or three leaf nodes. Leaves, roots and stems can be affected.

Appearance and effect of the disease

Damping off begins as a yellowish-brown discoloration on the lower portion of the stalk. Stems have brown lesions and eventually a dark reddish-brown sunken canker. Cankers form mostly on the stems, between nodes. The third, fourth and fifth nodes are affected most frequently. As the disease progresses, the lower part of the stem becomes soft and brown. Eventually, the underdeveloped plant simply falls over.

The wilting may resemble root rot when the plant first starts to wilt and the leaves turn yellow, but stem canker has not yet appeared. The key difference from root rot is that in damping off the roots are not affected.

In the later stages of damping off in vegetative seedlings, the leaves droop and turn yellow. As lesions extend up the plant, it begins to wilt due to vascular damage (see the entry on Pythium for more information about this).

Damping off can easily be mistaken for excessive fertilization (nutrient burn), high levels of salts in the soil, nutrient solution buildup in hydroponic systems, excessive heat or cold or excessive or insufficient soil moisture. A key diagnostic sign is the brown discoloration near the soil line.

Prevention

The best preventives for damping off all focus on keeping the soil from getting too wet. Although it is always possible to overwater, these measures greatly reduce damping off. Use a porous well-draining soil with large enough particles to have air spaces between them. Soggy, muddy or mucky soil or planting mixes have particles that are very fine. They hold too much water so the roots are deprived of oxygen.

Use a planting mix that includes a generous amount of larger-size particles. This creates a well-draining mix without excess water and with sufficient air for the roots.

Let the soil surface dry before watering. Use a moisture meter to test soil moisture. Testing the soil near the edge of the pot is less likely to disturb root development. The deeper the container, the more likely that lower levels have a higher moisture level than the top of the container. Make sure to use a planting mix with large-enough particles to drain well.

Place the seeds no deeper than 0.25 inch. Soil is wetter farther down.

Use sterile soil or planting mix to minimize chance of an infection.

Apply a fungicide to seeds before planting to minimize post-emergence damping off. Don't transplant seedlings outside until they have several sets of leaves. Younger plants don't have a robust resistance to disease.

Properly aged compost, and tea made from compost, help protect plants from all sorts of fungal infections.

Keep the grow room and tools clean, and keep the plants free of pests. This helps to prevent damping off just as it helps against other fungal diseases.

- *Bacillus subtilis* (beneficial bacteria)
- *Gliocladium* (beneficial fungus)
- *Pseudomonas* (beneficial bacteria)
- *Streptomyces griseoviridis* (beneficial bacteria)

Control

There is very little chance of saving seedlings that are struck by damping off soon after they germinate. Vegetative-stage plants with a few sets of leaves have a better chance of fighting it off with the help of a fungicide.

Catching the problem early makes your growing life easier. As with other fungal diseases, remove infected areas of the plant entirely and treat the resulting wounds with hydrogen peroxide (H_2O_2). If the stem canker becomes severe, then foliar feeding is a must to maintain the plants' vigor, strength and stamina for the fight.

- Clove oil
- Copper oil
- Coriander oil
- Quaternary amines
- Sesame oil
- *Trichoderma* (beneficial fungi)

Wilted plant

Section 4

ENVIRONMENTAL STRESSES

Temperature, humidity, air quality and the amount and type of light all affect your garden's health and yield. Whether growing indoors or outdoors, the grower must do as much as possible to optimize the environment the plants grow in. The problems discussed in this section are mainly caused by grower error. You get details on how to fix each mistake and how to avoid its recurrence.

INDICAS AND SATIVAS

Most commonly grown strains of cannabis are sativa, indica or a hybrid of the two. Sativas have long, skinny leaves; indicas have short, fat, stubby leaves. You can tell by looking at the plant whether the plant has more sativa or indica. Sativa-dominants have long, thin finger-shaped leaves coming from the petiole. Indica-dominants have broader, slightly shorter leaves. Indicas are darker green. Both adapt differently to certain environmental factors. Indoor-adapted indicas can bleach from intense light. Sativas can handle more intense light. Sativas take much longer to finish, while indicas ripen faster.

Plant with airy buds

AIRY, LOOSE BUDS

Problem: The buds are airy and loose.

Solution: Airy, loose buds are caused by lack of light, high temperature during their growth period or lack of nutrients.

Indoors, high temperature in the garden space or just near the light causes the buds to grow airy and lanky. Move the buds farther from the light so the temperature of the leaf is no higher than 860. Measure the temperature using a surface temperature thermometer, which uses laser light to measure the temperature of solid surfaces. Adjust the temperature in the growing space and canopy to maintain the leaf temperature.

Outdoors, high temperature during flowering results in loose buds. This is not usually a problem when plants flower in autumn, when the temperature cools. However, when they flower early (because they are early-flowering varieties or because of forcing using light deprivation), this may be a problem.

One solution is to lower the temperature in the outdoor garden using a micro-sprayer system often used to cool outdoor living spaces. A powerful pump or high water pressure creates an ultra-fine spray, consisting of droplets that are five microns or less. These evaporate, lowering air temperature in the immediately surrounding area without leaving any moisture on the plants. Micro-spray cleaners are commonly used in greenhouses and patios. They use small amounts of water and are easy to install and operate. There are many types of water coolers.

Many greenhouses use "waterwalls," which trickle water through porous fiber. Air blown through the fiber is cooled as it enters the greenhouse.

Plants that are not receiving enough light during flowering grow airy buds that don't dense up and mature incompletely. The lighter-weight buds are not as potent because they develop fewer trichomes, which are not as large as they would be under full light.

Nutritionally, calcium, potassium, magnesium and silica can improve airy buds. Plants that don't receive enough Potassium during flowering cannot grow abundant flowers. Increase Potassium during mid and late flowering.

Loose airy buds

BROKEN STEMS AND BRANCHES

Problem: Sometimes stems that are heavy with buds tear away from the plant at the joint where the stem and branch are attached, especially during rain or windstorms. Another problem is that some varieties have a weak spot at the joint and some of the lower branches tear away as a matter of course.

Solution: Broken stems and branches that are still attached to the plant can often be repaired using a splint to keep the parts together and for support. Realign the two pieces and tape each part to the support. A stick, piece of wood or other strong material can be used as a splint.

Use twist ties or tape to support branches tearing away from the plant. Wrap it around the canopy to keep branches from falling.

Plants can be protected from breaking by wrapping a plastic net or chicken wire loosely around them so that neither wind nor rain can pull or tear the branches. For small plants, use tomato cages. Supporting the stem using a sturdy stake keeps the plant upright and relieves the stem of additional pressure.

CLONES

Problem: The cuttings won't root.

Solution: Rooting machines make it easy to root cuttings. However, rooting cuttings is not difficult. Trim healthy cuttings from desirable plants. They should be between 6 and 8 inches (15 and 20 cm) long. Trim off most of the leaves, making sure to leave the top leaves on. Dip the cutting in rooting gel or powder and then stick it in sterile soil or planting mix, rock wool or Oasis® cubes. Keep the temperature at about 72-75°F0 (22-24°C). The roots will appear in 8 to12 days. If you are only rooting a few clones, you might try rooting them in water.

To keep the medium sterile and increase oxygen in the water, which promotes rooting; make a solution of 1 part drugstore hydrogen peroxide (3%) with 5 parts water. Initially, give the cuttings 10 watts of cool white fluorescent per square foot. The clones should be kept in a space with 65% humidity or higher. A dome or cover is an easy way to maintain high humidity. Remove covers after five or six days, and keep the clones in an area with high humidity.

After about five days, add flowering formula fertilizer at one-quarter strength.

Increase the light intensity to 20 watts per square foot. Over the next 10 days increase the strength of the nutrients by adding grow formula. The roots should be visible within two weeks of starting.

Varieties differ in how easily and how long they take to root.

Algae can also gunk up clones growing in water, impeding their growth. To prevent this, use a dark-colored opaque container to hold the water. Use distilled or RO water if possible.

Problem: Can I take cuttings from a flowering plant? What about a ripe plant?

Solution: Flowering plants, even ripe ones, can be cloned. If possible, take the cutting from a shaded area so that the bud isn't as developed as the outside buds. Woody stems should be avoided when picking clones; the harder the stem, the harder it is for the clone to root. Trim as much of the flower off as you can while leaving green leaves on the cutting. Set the cutting in the medium. Keep the light on continuously. It will start to root, and the new upper growth will be vegetative rather than flowers.

ELONGATED SEEDLINGS

See *Stretching*.

Light burn

FLUORESCENT BURN

Problem: A few of the plant's leaves were touching the fluorescent light and they are burned.

Solution: When using fluorescents, keep the plants 6 inches (about 5 cm) below the tubes. Without regular attention, the leaves will touch the lights as they grow. If they are not moved from the plant, the leaves will brown where they were touching the light and exposed to the heat. Occasional light damage won't harm the plant. If the leaf is no longer viable, remove it from the plant. If leaf burn happens regularly, place a wire barrier around the tube so the leaves cannot touch the lamp.

FORCING FLOWERING

Problem: Forcing flowering is not working. The plants won't flower even though the light cycle was turned to 12 hours darkness/12 hours of light several weeks ago.

Solution: Plants aren't flowering because the light has remained on, there are light leaks into the room or the light was turned on several times during the dark period. If you have to go into the garden during the dark period, use a green light in the garden without interrupting the light cycle.

To search for light pollution, go inside the room when all the lights are off. Once your eyes adjust, look for stray light entering the room. It might be affecting flowering. Block it.

GROW ROOM CONDITIONS

HUMID GROW SPACE

Problem: The grow space is very humid.

Solution: The garden space is humid because the plants emit moisture. It is accumulating in the garden space, and water is evaporating from the containers. Sloppy watering may be another source of humidity.

The moisture must be removed. One way is to ventilate it out and replace it with drier air. If the garden is a closed system, use a dehumidifier, which condenses moisture from the air. The problem with dehumidifiers is that they release heat and can make the space too hot. The hot air is exhausted out of the space.

If the room is already running hot, an air conditioner can be used to remove the moisture as it cools the garden.

HOT GROW ROOM

Problem: The grow room is too hot.

Solutions: There are a few ways to cool down a hot grow space.
- It can be ventilated to remove the heat.
- An air conditioner can be used to remove the heat from the air.
- Before flowering, an air cooler that evaporates water to cool the room can be used if the space has low humidity. It does not add too much moisture and can be used during vegetative growth. An air cooler is very efficient. However, the unit may create too much moisture for the flowering stage.

- If there is a big drop in temperature at night, many of the heat problems may be solved by running the garden lights at night, rather than during the day.
- If the plants are being grown hydroponically, the water can be cooled. This keeps the entire plant cool even though the air is hot. If the room temperature is in the high 80s (27-30°C), keep the water temperature in the 60s (15-20° C). Aquarium water chillers can be installed in the system to cool the water as it passes through the line.
- Remove all heat-producing equipment from the grow room if possible, especially light ballasts and large pumps, and place them in a separated ventilated space.
- The best way to deal with heat is to prevent it from getting into the garden to begin with. Using air-cooled lights keeps the heat generated by the lamps from entering the garden. Tubes carry it from the lamps to the outside without affecting room air temperature.

Hermaphrodite

HERMAPHRODITES

Problem: I have a plant that grew fine outside. I took cuttings and grew the plants indoors. Unlike the outdoor plant, the indoor plant turned hermaphroditic. How can I prevent this?

Solution: The plant is adapted to outdoor conditions. Growing indoors produces stress and the plant turns hermaphroditic. We know no solutions to this. Clones from plants grown indoors may exhibit hermaphrodite tendencies as part of an intergenerational, nongenetic, but chromosomal, adaptation process.

Problem: I am growing six varieties in my outdoor garden, which I started

Hermaphrodite

from stash seeds. Three of the plants are hermaphroditic. Why? What should I do about it?

Solution: The hermaphroditic plants are sometimes genetically programmed to be that way. That's how you got the stash seeds in the first place; the buds were self-fertilized and produced the seeds you planted.

You could try picking the male flowers, but that can be time-consuming and is usually only partially successful, since it is so easy to miss a few flowers. If the plants are heavily laden with male flowers, removing the plants might be the best way to ensure that the other plants remain seed-free.

In the future, use seeds that have a known heritage.

Problem: I have a hermaphroditic plant. She didn't have any male flowers until the third week of flowering, and they are all on an occasional branch, not interspersed. If I use the pollen from this plant to produce seed, will they be hermaphroditic?

Solution: Most of the plants resulting from the plant crossing itself will be hermaphroditic. At least some of the plants from outcrosses of the pollen or by importing pollen to cross with the hermaphrodite will produce some hermaphrodites. To simplify your life, this plant should not be used for reproductive purposes.

KNOCKED-DOWN PLANT

Problem: The plant was knocked down during a storm or by animals.

Solution: The plant must be picked up, supported and tied up to keep it upright. First make all the preparations. Position the support stakes and have the rope or tape ready. Gently lift the plant into position and hold it steady as it is tied up. Three or four stakes spaced around the plant or stem provide greater support than a single stake tied to the stem. With a single stake, more stress is placed on the stem-plant joint, sometimes resulting in stem breaks.

To prevent further damage, encircle the plant with plastic netting or chicken wire.

If appropriate, such as after a dry windstorm, water the plant.

If the roots were torn from the earth, cover them by adding more planting medium and gently packing it around. Make sure all the roots are well covered by a thick layer of soil so they are protected from the air. Water using Super-Thrive or a B-12 rooting compound and use humic acid to help with the roots' trauma.

Sometimes it is unfeasible to raise the plant upright because of damage to the stem and branches. Still, the plant branches should be raised off the ground using shipping pallets or sawhorses. Use plastic netting to help support them.

Once the plant dries out and has been stabilized, usually after a few days, it can be washed free of dirt using a gentle water spray. This should be done only on a warm sunny day early enough so the plant will dry completely by nightfall. Don't do this on cool or cloudy days because the moisture promotes mold growth. Place a rug under the plant to protect the buds from debris and mud.

LIGHT

Plants use light as energy. Chloroplasts, which are special organs inside leaf cells, capture light from a rainbow of the spectrum and use it to power photosynthesis. In this process, plants take elements from water and air and make sugar, while releasing free oxygen. Sugar is used to fuel metabolism, the process of living, and to build tissue, including flowers. The more light the plants have, the faster the chloroplasts function. As long as the plant is supplied with enough water, CO_2 and nutrients, it increases production when it receives more light. This results in faster growth and larger yield.

Outdoors, plants thrive in full sun. Indoors, for full tight buds, indicas need at least 40 watts of HPS light per square foot. Sativas need at least 60 watts. HPS lamps can be used both for vegetative growth and during flowering. Double-ended HPS and ceramic metal halide lamps are more efficient than HPS lamps.

NO FLOWERS

Symptom: Plants won't flower indoors.

Solution: Indoors, marijuana plants are induced to flower when the uninterrupted dark period lasts 12 hours for four or five days. Then most varieties require a continuation of that regimen. The light deprivation should start and end at the same time each day. For this reason, the lights should be set on a timer and not depend on human reliability. See also *Forcing Flowering*.

DARK CYCLE INTERRUPTED

Problem: The lights were left on for one or more days.

Symptom: If the lights were on for only a day, there won't be much effect. However, if the lights were on for several days, the plants may start reverting to vegetative growth during early stages of flowering. Light pollution has less of an effect as the buds get closer to maturity.

Solution: Return the garden to its usual cycle immediately. This will prevent any further damage. If there has been any reversion to vegetative growth, the buds will take a little longer to mature. There may be a slight reduction in yield.

Problem: The lights were left off for one or more days.

Symptom: Bud ripening may be hastened.

Solution: Turn the lights back on and maintain the regular flowering schedule until buds are ripe. Keeping plants in the dark makes them far more susceptible to diseases. Keep the space warm and with a humidity no higher than 50%.

Problem: The lights were turned on and off at irregular times.

Symptoms: Lanky, irregular bud growth. Hermaphroditism also occurs in some cases. See Hermaphrodites for more information.

Solution: Start using a timer to keep a strict light regimen and help the buds grow and gain potency.

LIGHT BURN

See *High Temperature: Tip burn.*

Nutrient burn

NUTRIENT BURN

Symptom: Very deep green leaves indicate an overabundance of Nitrogen. Tip burn may indicate too much Potassium. Severe overfertilization results in wilting.

Solution: Stop fertilizing. Immediately flush the medium with pH-adjusted unfertilized water. Time is a factor. The faster the problem is solved, the less likely that plant death will occur.

Sometimes plants appear to be suffering from a nutrient deficiency, but treatment fails to solve the problem. It could be an excess of nutrients. This creates chemical reactions that lock up nutrients, making them insoluble and preventing them from being absorbed by the roots. When this occurs, flush the plant with twice the amount of water as the size of the container.

Photosynthesis Plus is a complete ecosystem in a bottle that is a growth enhancer function at the foliar level and the root zone. Helping to speed uptake and distribution of macro- and micro- nutrients that are required for plant metabolism.

No two nutrient burns are alike; they have different symptoms and mimic different problems. If you have added nutrients and the problems persist, flush the containers and lower the nutrient concentration. Feed plants according to their size. Large plants use more nutrients than smaller ones.

It is always best to dilute fertilizer solutions and gradually increase concentrations. If you add too much, you may have to flush.

Nutrient burn

169

PRUNING: BRANCHES

Problem: Should I prune my plants? How?

Solution: Pruning plants increases yield and decreases height while helping the stem to grow stronger and stouter. The center bud, which is the tallest part of the plant, has apical dominance. It produces auxin, a chemical that inhibits growth of other buds. When the top bud is cut, the side buds that surround the top bud start to grow vigorously. As a result, instead of growing one jumbo and several medium-size buds, several very large buds develop. They weigh more in total than the unpruned buds.

Pruning repeatedly results in numerous small buds. These are more tedious to manicure than a few big buds.

Indoors, the best time to prune is about 10 to 15 days before the plants are forced to flower. Outdoors, pruning should be done several weeks before the plants are expected to flower. To top the plant, cut off the new growth on the central branch near the top.

Sometimes it is more convenient to have a bushy plant with small- or medium-size buds than one with fewer, larger buds. To produce a plant that looks bushy, cut the top growth after the plant develops about five sets of leaves. The plant will develop four or more large side branches to replace the center growth. When these branches have developed four or five sets of leaves, prune off the top growth of each branch. The plant develops numerous branches as a result.

PRUNING: LEAVES

Problem: Should the fan leaves be pruned from plants? If so, when?

Solution: Leaves are sugar factories. Specialized organs in leaf cells use the energy from light to combine carbon dioxide and oxygen to make sugar and release oxygen to the environment. The sugar is used to fuel the plant's metabolism and as a building block for new tissue. The plant spends energy to grow the leaf. Once it is grown, a leaf is a net energy generator. When leaves are picked, the plant is deprived of an energy generator and does not grow as quickly as when it is left unpruned. For this reason, leaves should not be pruned from plants in vegetative growth and early stages of flowering.

There are only a few stages when leaves should be removed. The first is in mid to late flowering. When a leaf covers or hides a bud from light, especially direct sunlight, it should be manipulated into another position if possible, but if not, it should be removed. It is more important that the growing buds get light than the leaf produces sugars.

As the flowers mature and the plant is using flowering formula nutrients, which contain little or no nitrogen, the plant transfers it from the leaves to the buds. The leaves turn yellow and are of little use to the plant. They snap from the stem with the slightest pressure.

The last stage when leaves should be removed is during manicuring.

SEED GERMINATION

Problem: How do I germinate seeds?

Solution: To hasten germination and kill infectious agents, soak the seed for 12 hours in a 1% hydrogen peroxide or compost tea solution. Place the seeds in sterile planting mix, pasteurized soil, planting pellets, rock wool or Oasis® cubes about 0.25 inch deep. Water using a 0.5% hydrogen peroxide solution with bloom fertilizer added at one-quarter strength. Keep the medium moist. To ensure constant humidity, cover the plant with a dome and keep it out of the sun. Keep the medium at about 72°F (22°C). The seeds should germinate in 2 to 10 days. Old seeds take longer to germinate than younger ones. Keep a strong light on the seedlings or they will stretch.

Outdoors, the seeds should be planted at about the same time corn is planted by gardeners in your area. The season can be hastened using row covers, but this may cause vegetative growth/flowering problems if a critical dark period is involved. This sometimes occurs when plants are placed outdoors early in the season.

The seeds should be planted about 0.25 inch (6 mm) deep on tilled soil or drilled into untilled soil. They require protection from overgrowing weeds. Once they reach unobstructed sunlight, they will soon dominate the canopy.

FEMINIZED PLANTS

Symptom: Do feminized seeds work? Do they produce all-female plants or hermaphrodites?

Solution: All-female seeds do work. They are produced by inducing male flowers in female plants using chemicals or environmental techniques. They eliminate the need for sexing.

Occasionally, a plant is hermaphroditic. This is the result of the technique that is used to produce hermaphrodites. When breeders use induced hermaphrodites in their breeding programs, rather than just for the last cross, they inadvertently select for hermaphroditism. Choose seeds from companies that enjoy a good reputation for these seeds.

SHORT GROWING SEASON

Problem: The plants I want to grow won't mature in time where I live.

Symptom: Immature buds at harvest.

Solution: Grow a different variety that does mature in time. Alternatively, force flowering early by covering the plants each day so they receive 12 hours of uninterrupted darkness. For instance, if you start covering the plants on July 20, varieties that take eight weeks to ripen will be ready to pick by September 15. Starting forcing on June 20 results in ripe buds on August 15.

SMALL PLANTS NOT GROWING

Symptom: The garden has bright light, is watered regularly and is being fertilized as directed, but the plant leaves are very dark colored and the plants grow very slowly.

Solution: If the plants are receiving adequate amounts of light, nutrients and water, the pH is probably out of range. This prevents the plants from utilizing the nutrients. Without nutrients the plant cannot make use of the light to create sugars for growth.

Solve the problem by adjusting the pH of the nutrient water solution to the range of 5.8-6.2. The easiest way to do this is by using pH Up or Down. These are very acid or alkaline powders and solutions, and very little is required to affect water pH. Hydrated and liquefied lime also works well in planting mediums.

Stretched seedlings

STRETCHING

Symptom: Plants with stems that stretch are problematic in the grow room and in outdoor gardens when height is an issue.

Solution: There are several reasons why plants stretch. The first is that they are genetically programmed to grow long stems between leaf sets. Sativa varieties that grow tall outside also grow long stems indoors. Genetics aside, there are a few things that a gardener can do to shorten the stem length between the leaves.

Plants stretch most with a combination of high temperature and low light levels. The plants stretch in an attempt to find more light. With lower tempera-

Stretched seedling

tures, they don't stretch as much. With high light levels, plants' needs are met so they don't stretch.

Strong air circulation that creates stem and leaf movement also strengthens and widens the stem as it slows vertical growth. When the wind bends the stem, it creates tiny tears in the tissue. The plant quickly repairs these tears by growing new tissue, strengthening the stem and increasing its diameter. Brushing and bending the plant leaves and stem a couple of times a day also helps with this.

The light spectrum can help control height. Blue light promotes shorter, stouter stems. Red and orange light promotes longer thinner stems.

Heat affects stem growth, too. Plants grow longer stems as the temperature rises. At about 600F (15°C) plant growth slows, but the stems tend to be thicker. At 800F (27°C) plants start to stretch. Both buds and lower stems are affected.

Sometimes buds that are close to a light grow airy or lanky. Growers erroneously attribute this to "light burn." However, this is not the problem. The difficulty is that the heat produced by the lamp is creating a very hot environment in the bud zone. There are several solutions to heat problems. Raising the lights is often the easiest. Air-cooled lamps prevent much of the heat from entering the room.

Temperature inversion is a method sometimes used in commercial greenhouses. When the temperature is higher during the dark period than the lighted period, vertical stem growth slows, resulting in stronger, thicker stems.

Lack of light causes stem elongation. Under low light conditions, seedlings and older plants grow long, thin stems attempting to reach more light. To stop stem stretching, provide a more intense light or lower the temperature. If seedlings have already stretched, support the stems using wooden skewers. Once they are given brighter light, the stems will fill out and will be able to support themselves. Older plants suffering from light deprivation stretch toward the light. Buds grow airy, don't tighten up and have sparse trichome coverage. Provide more light, either by adding additional bulbs or by placing the light closer to the plants.

Pruning can be used to shorten stem length. Removing the top of the main stem forces growth of the surrounding branches. These branches do not grow as long or as tall as the main stem. Bending the top branch until it creases and hangs low also spurs lower stem growth. The branch may need a crutch to support it and hold it in place until the plant's new growth heals the wound.

TEMPERATURE

LOW TEMPERATURE

Indoors, marijuana grows fastest at a temperature of about 800F (21 to 23°C) during the lit period and a temperature drop of no more than 15°F (9°C) to 650F (15°C) at the lowest during the dark period. Keeping the same temperature or raising it during the dark period helps prevent stretching. Plants enriched with CO_2 will yield more at a slightly higher temperature of 860F (27°C).

When leaf temperature drops to 600F (15°C) during the lit period, plant growth virtually stops and yields suffer. Cool temperatures for a few nights won't make too much of a difference, but if they persist throughout the flowering period, they can create a serious problem with yield. This may not be noticeable if you unfamiliar with the garden's usual level of production.

Solution: Use a CO_2 generator or an electric heater to heat the space.

During cold weather, if the floor can be kept warm, at 80oF (27°C), the heated roots will help the stems and leaves to withstand cold air. If you have only a few plants, use a plant heating mat. Larger gardens can be heated using a recirculating hot water heater. If you are heating hydroponic water, you must oxygenate it so the roots don't drown. Hot water holds far less Oxygen (O), which cools water, so heated water must be supplemented with O. Aquarium bubblers help. Oxygenators pump pure O into the water or make it using electrolysis of water.

An all natural CO_2 generator is The Enhancer from TBN Naturals. Safe and effective for CO_2 supplementation that can reach 1200 PPM in a 12x12x12 area for up to two weeks, no additional equipment needed. The Enhancer now comes in a convenient refill pack where the contents of the Refill Pack can be added and instantly CO_2 is once again available for use.

Outdoors, most varieties can withstand temperatures as low as 50°F (10°C) without problems. But 50°F is not an ideal temperature, since it slows growth of tissue built using sugars produced during the day and slows down photosynthesis and tissue growth when it occurs during the day. Temperatures below 40°F (4°C) often result in tissue damage.

Solutions: Gas patio heaters can keep the plants in a garden warm on chilly nights. Keeping the temperature at 60°F increases plant growth.

Outdoors, a sheet of polyethylene plastic secured over a simple frame keeps the temperature up and protects the garden from wind and rain. A heater provides even more protection.

Light burn

HIGH TEMPERATURE

Symptom: Elongated stems and airy roots.

Plants can withstand high temperature as long as they have a large root system that can draw up enough water to keep the plant cool through transpiration. During vegetative growth, temperatures in the high 80s and higher result in stem elongation. During flowering, high temperatures result in airy buds. This occurs both indoors and out.

Solutions: Indoors, lower the temperature by using ventilation or air-conditioning or by eliminating heat from the garden using air-cooled lights. Remember that the air temperature in the aisles of a room isn't important; it's the temperature under the lights, at the plant canopy level, that affects the plants. Use a surface temperature thermometer to check plant temperature at the top of the canopy. Adjust the room temperature based on canopy temperature.

Outdoors, cool the air using micro-sprayers that lower the temperature 20 to 30 degrees during day. They emit a spray with droplets that are 5 microns or smaller. The droplets evaporate, cooling the ambient air.

Symptom: Wilting plants in the afternoon.

Outdoors, plants in small pots or small planting holes surrounded by bad soil have a hard time even when the soil is kept moist. This is because they don't have enough roots to draw water to the leaves. If they are in containers, they may also be overheated each day as their black planting containers absorb light energy and transform it into heat.

Solutions: Check to see if the plant is root-bound. If it is, then transplant it to a larger container. If the containers are dark-colored, paint or cover them so they are light colored and reflect most of the light.

Symptom: Tip burn.

Symptom: The buds closest to the lights are stretching and look bleached.

Solutions: The space near the lights is too hot. This effect is sometimes misdiagnosed as too bright a light. The buds can take the intense light: it's the heat that is affecting them.

Keep the lights farther away from the plants.

Install air-cooled lights with reflectors to reduce the heat near the light.

Generally speaking, 1,000-watt lights should be kept about 3 feet (1 m) from the plant tops. Air-cooling lights can be spaced 18-24 inches (45-60 cm) away.

Lights can be moved closer if they are placed on light movers.

WATER

Example of a wilting plant vs. a healthy plant

WHEN TO WATER

Marijuana roots should never dry out. When they do, the plant wilts. If the plants are in soil or planting mix, water when the medium feels as though it is losing its moisture. Waiting for it to dry out before watering, even if the plant does not show signs of wilting, deprives the plant of water it would use for growth. Use a water meter. The probe provides information on water levels deeper into the planting medium.

The amount of water that a plant needs and how often it should be watered depend on its size, the size of the container, canopy, root level, room temperature, humidity and the stage of growth.

- Larger plants require more water.
- Larger containers need to be watered less frequently.
- When the temperature is warmer, plants require more water.
- When the humidity is higher, plants need to be watered less frequently.
- During the last few weeks of flowering, plants use less water.

Outdoors, during the hot days of summer, soils often dry out quickly and may need to be watered quite a bit. Adding compost and water-holding crystals to the soil at planting time can help it hold water for longer periods.

Covering the soil with mulch slows water evaporation dramatically. Compost, wood chips, hay or dried leaves, newspapers and even rugs can be used.

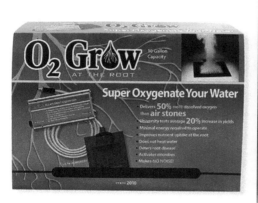

O_2 Grow elevates dissolved oxygen levels by manufacturing 100% pure oxygen to increase the speed of plant growth, root ball size, nutrient uptake, and the number and size of flowers by balancing the pH, preventing root disease, and promoting beneficial bacteria. The product can be used with standard electrical hook ups as well as solar power. O_2 Grow oxygenators are designed for 10 to 250 gallon capacities.

DROWNING ROOTS

Symptoms: No discoloration. Drooping, but not wilted, leaves have an unhealthy, fatigued look. Very slow, if any, growth.

Problem: Overwatering can create an anaerobic condition, which is a lack of oxygen (O). Roots don't use carbon dioxide (CO_2), but they do use O. They obtain it from the air spaces between the soil particles or from the O dissolved in the water. When they are deprived of O, they cannot function properly and gradually lose their vigor. The roots are easily attacked by pathogens.

INDOOR PROBLEMS

There are three possible causes of drowning roots indoors.

- You are watering too often and the planting mix is not getting a chance to drain.
- There are no drainage holes in the bottom of the container or they are clogged.
- The soil or planting mix's particles are too small and don't have enough air spaces between them. To test this, water the mix. Once it is saturated, it should drain freely. Mixes that drain slowly have too tight a texture.

Solutions: Make sure the container has working drainage holes. If not, cut some into the container using a knife, drill or thermal tool.

If the planting mix has fine particles, water less frequently. Use a coarser, more aerated planting mix if you are transplanting and with future crops.

OUTDOOR PROBLEMS

Outdoors, clay and rain-saturated soils are the usual causes of poor drainage. Sandy soils, on the other hand, may drain too well.

ORGANIC SOLUTION

SUPERCHAR

A proprietary blend of biochar from bamboo, worm castings, humic acid from leonardite, crab shell, rock dust

"happy plants start with happy soil"

A blend of biochar, premium worm castings, humate, rock dust and crab shell Superchar will hydrate the mix with worm casting extract. This long term soil amendment improves moisture retention and soil structure.

SOIL

CLAY SOILS

Problem: Clay soils are notorious for drainage problems. They form a virtually nonporous layer so the water just puddles. This creates an anaerobic condition that damages the roots.

Solution: Before planting, the clay should be dug up. Soils that are composed of clay but with substantial amounts of other materials can be modified using compost, fresh organic matter, sand, perlite or used planting mix. Gypsum and sulfur are sometimes used to modify clay chemically. Both act to break up its tight molecular structure but work slowly. Their full impact occurs over several seasons.

Soils that are almost all clay are very difficult to garden. Alternatives are creating a raised bed or containers to hold soil above ground, or excavating the clay and replacing it with different soil. In areas that become saturated from rain during the growing season, use mounds or raised beds to keep the roots comfortably above the water level. If you are digging planting holes, try to reach a permeable layer. You might use an auger bit on a drill to create a drainage hole that reaches a permeable layer.

SANDY SOILS

Sandy soils don't hold water. Instead it drains, quickly leaving the plants thirsty if water isn't supplied quite often, sometimes even several times a day. To increase the soil's water-holding qualities, add compost and other decayed plant matter. This may require moving a lot of material and may not be feasible. Water-holding crystals also help.

Irrigate over a period of time using small amounts of water such as a drip. This way the ground is kept evenly moist. When it is watered all at once, it drains and after a short time the soil is moisture deficient. One simple solution is to use water containers that have adjustable spigots. Adjust the spigot to a steady drip, so it drips the whole day. Those steady drops will keep the plant from getting thirsty. Don't water at night because the water may drain below the root level. Instead, irrigate during the day when the plant is using it.

Another solution is to create a water-holding planting hole. Place a deep plastic tray or tarp in the bottom of the hole and fill it with water-absorbing material such as coir or wood chips. With rain or watering the tray or tarp will act as an underground reservoir and keep water from draining too quickly.

CannaLot Medicinal Megasoil is a specialty soil mix that contains a wide variety of mineral, plant and animal based organic fertilizers, biochar, crustacean meal, and wollastonite in a base of compost, worm castings, coir and peat. The soil will maximize performance without signs of N or P overdose.

DRIED-OUT SOIL

Add a wetting agent to the water to prevent it from beading on the surface of the soil. Wetting agents allow water to be easily absorbed into the soil and are available at garden shops. Gardeners sometimes use soap or detergents as wetting agents, but much better products natural and organic products are available.

Watering

UNDERWATERING: WILTED PLANTS

Symptom: Plants grow slowly, wilting.

Solution: Water the plants. If they are wilted, do not use fertilizer-enriched water. Use unenriched but pH-adjusted water. After they have perked up, you can reinstitute the fertilizer program.

If the amount of water is just barely adequate to maintain the plants, growth slows. This may be hard to notice. However, once the plants receive more generous supplies of water, provided they have enough nutrients, they will experience a growth spurt.

CHLORINE IN WATER

Problem: The irrigation water has large amounts of chlorine. Does this have a bad effect on the plants?

Solution: Chlorine affects plants in several ways. First, in media systems it kills some of the microorganisms that form a community with the roots in the rhizosphere. This results in slower growth. Some leaf tip burn may be the result of excess chlorine, but this is rare. It is most likely to happen during hot sunny days when the plant uses a lot of water.

Most gardeners water straight from the tap, which most likely has been treated with chlorine and possibly fluoride. In spite of these chemicals in the water, plants grow well. They may grow better with unchlorinated water. Most city water is chlorinated with chloramines, which cannot be removed by boiling or allowing the water to stand. If you wish to dechlorinate tap water, activated carbon filters will do the job. There are also specialized UV systems designed specifically for dechlorination. A number of chemical dechlorinators are available for use in fish ponds and aquariums. These products are safe for fish and plants; however, the author has not tried them and cannot say for certain which works best in marijuana gardens.

HARD OR SOFT WATER

Symptoms: Erratic deficiencies and growth problems.

Solution: Check water for dissolved solids. It should be between 100 and150 parts per million (ppm). Water that is too low (soft water) should be adjusted to 150 ppm using Cal-Mag solution. Water that is too high, with over 250 ppm dissolved solids, should be filtered using ionic or reverse osmosis filters.

Hard water prevents balanced nutrient uptake. Filtered water can be mixed with unfiltered to create water suitable for plants. Water in a Los Angeles suburb measured 450 ppm dissolved solids. After filtered through an ionic filter, it had a ppm of 13. The gardener mixed 1 part of unfiltered water to 2 parts filtered, resulting in a solids level in the mixed water of just above 150 ppm. The water has the right amount of dissolved solids for use in a nutrient water solution.

Hard-water deposits can damage hydroponic/aeroponic systems.

SODIUM IN WATER

Avoid any water that contains high levels of sodium. Plants absorb Sodium (Na) first, before any other element. It causes the plant's vascular system to break down.

For this reason, water treated with water softeners should be avoided.

SULFUR IN WATER

Water with a sulfurous odor should be checked for its pH. Sulfur is acidic and the water may have a very low pH. Try avoiding use of this water. If you must use it, adjust its with pH Up. Soils that have been irrigated with the water may also be affected and have a low pH, indicating acidity. These soils should also be tested and adjusted if necessary using lime, which raises the pH.

WATER TEMPERATURE

Problem: What temperature should I keep my hydroponic water?

Solution: In a garden with a canopy at normal temperature of no higher than 80°F (24°C), keep the water at about 68-72°F (22-23°C). If the canopy temperature is higher, then lower the water temperature a few degrees.

The problem with warm water is that it holds little oxygen (O), which the roots require. O supplementation of the water can raise its temperature.

WEATHER

COLD SPELLS

Problem: The weather report says that we are going to experience a cold spell that will dip below freezing. This is to be followed by warmer weather later in the month. How do I prepare my garden for the cold?

Solution: The idea here is to keep the plants alive until the weather changes. If the temperature can be kept at 45°F (7°C) for a short time, the plants will survive with little damage. When higher temperatures return, the plants will start growing again.

If the plants can be moved inside and given moderate light on cycle, they can be preserved for a few days until the outside weather changes.

A patio heater can be placed in the garden and may provide enough heat to keep the plant from frostbite. A temporary greenhouse constructed of wood frame and plastic will preserve the heat better and can be removed when better weather arrives.

Individual plants can be wrapped using polyethylene. This protects the plants from wind and preserves some heat. However, the cold will eventually get to the plants unless there is some source of heat for them. Forced-air heaters can deliver heat to the plants. Make sure to set the gauge at about 70°F (21°C) so the plants do not overheat.

COOL WEATHER

Problem: The plants are not mature and the weather is getting cooler. How long can the plants stay outside?

Solution: Plant growth slows dramatically as the daylight temperature slips down into the low 60s (15-18°C) and virtually stops in the mid-50s (12-14°C). If it is unlikely that the temperature will rise to the high 60s or 70s (above 20°C), then it may be useless to keep the plants growing.

At the same time, the evening temperature may be slipping dangerously low. The plants can withstand temperatures in the 40s F (5-10°C), but when it slips into the 30s (below 4°C), tissue damage is likely.

The solution depends on the amount of sunlight available. As autumn turns closer to winter the intensity of sunlight diminishes tremendously and its light reaches the earth at a lower (more oblique) angle. Often, plants that were in full light during summer and early autumn are shaded most of the time. Clouds may obscure the sun most of the time. The plants do not receive enough light energy to support growth. They should be harvested. If the buds are too immature to smoke, they can be processed for kief, extracts or cooking.

Another solution might be to install metal halide or HPS lamps over the plants in the garden.

If the plants are getting sunlight but are still experiencing cold weather, they could be protected using clear plastic hanging over a frame. The air inside the frame heats up, so growth is promoted.

One way to keep the air warm at night in enclosed spaces is to use passive heaters made by filling dark-colored containers with water. The containers heat up during the day, then radiate heat at night.

Patio heaters that use propane tanks can also keep the plants warm. Burning the gas produces CO_2 and water vapor. The extra CO_2 promotes plant growth.

HUMID WEATHER

Problem: The weather is turning humid.

Solution: Harvest all mature buds. Spray the plants with antifungals. Keep the plants on the warm side if possible.

If this weather is common during the ripening season, then plant varieties with looser buds that dry out more easily.

RAINY WEATHER

Problem: Rainy weather is forecast. How can the plants be protected?

Solution: Rainy weather promotes mold. Water gets into the buds and creates a perfect environment for molds such as Botrytis to grow. The buds hold the water and humidity in their crevices so it is hard to dry them out.

If the plants can be moved or a protective enclosure can be constructed, the plants will be protected from rain but not moisture. Raising the temperature of the enclosed area into the high 70s (24-26°C), beyond the optimal range for mold growth, may protect the plants and help dry out the buds. A fan circulating the hot air helps.

If the rain is expected to be brief, followed by warming dry weather, the plants can be protected by treating them with antifungals such as potassium bicarbonate or milk before the rain starts. If the forecast is for prolonged rain, the best solution may be to harvest the plants rather than risk them turning to mush.

WILTING

Problem: Wilting appears suddenly. One moment the plants are fine and a few minutes later wilting starts that can progress slowly or quickly.

Solution: Plants draw water up by keeping a higher salt concentration in their tissues than in the surrounding soil. If the salts (fertilizer nutrients) become more concentrated in the planting mix than the plant, either the plant can no longer draw up water or it actually drains from the plant. Use pH-adjusted water to flush the soil. Use water equal to about one and a half times the volume of the container, or about 7 gallons of water, to flush a 5-gallon container.

Cannabis leaves sometimes droop right at the end of the light period; this is not a cause for concern.

Photo by Mark Plonsky

Section 5

CONTROLS

In this section of the book we dig deeper into the major control methods discussed in chapters 1-4. You will be reminded as to whether the control is used to battle nutrient deficiencies, pests or diseases and be given specific instruction on how to use each control. Many solutions listed here can be used for more than one problem.

Outdoors, I use the term "control" to mean the elimination of noticeable damage to plants. Indoors, except in certain predator/prey situations, it means the elimination of the problem.

All of the controls listed here are safe to use for herb or for edible crops. Sprays are washed away by water, including rain, so plan to reapply spray products after rain or any watering that hits the affected areas of the plants. There are no products with hard-to-pronounce ingredients or with names that are a compilation of chemical terms. Most of the solutions use nature-designed chemistry (mostly plant oils) or natural processes to protect your garden.

THEORIES AND PRACTICES OF IPM

Integrated Pest Management combines the practice of pest and disease prevention, as well as planning protocols beforehand, with regular horticultural practices. The thinking is to consider pests and disease with every step you take as you garden.

Take into account biological controls first, organic or natural pesticides second and industrial pesticides or chemical controls third. It is important to note that in situations like full-blown mite infestation, the protocols you choose can and should be immediately moved forward to the chemical control phase. The idea is to consider the most beneficial outcome with the least amount of environmental impact. Sometimes that means stage 3 immediately because stages 1 and 2 will drag you into deeper waters.

In nurseries and greenhouses, an IPM chart or binder is often located with work logs or MSDS sheets. You probably don't need to write out a formal IPM plan especially because most of the meat is usually pest-specific as well as site and control protocol–specific. This book does a lot of that for you so realistically most growers can focus on planning safe and effective strategies to navigate most of the troubles commonly encountered. Practice at this will build a gardener's skills in dealing with new problems, pests or diseases on the fly.

General IPM checklists usually provide growers with a guide on how to conduct their search for garden issues as well as these specific protocols and countermeasure implementation plans. They all kind of go something like:

Step 1 Observe the environment.

Step 2 If temperature, humidity and irrigation are within range, inspect plants for vectors or symptoms.

Step 3 If you don't see no pests or symptoms, commence daily duties.

Step 4 If during daily gardening you notice a vector or symptom, then implement IPM procedures accordingly.

The pests, diseases, prevention techniques and control measures are all here in the guide for you to quickly access and use. When going through the motions, please consider Integrated Pest Management as a way to maximize efficiency in identifying problems quickly as well as taking the path of lesser environmental impact.

A GENERAL NOTE ON CONTROL PRODUCTS

Always read the label carefully before buying or using any control product. You need to follow the manufacturer's directions carefully to use these products safely and avoid harming the plants. You also need to identify the ingredients in a product to be sure that it will treat the problem you're dealing with and will not introduce additional problems you don't want. Many modern garden products seek to be all-in-one cures for common garden problems, for example, a micronutrient fertilizer that also contains high levels of nitrogen. Others apply more than one control for the same problem, such as a pyrethrum product that also contains rotenone or piperonyl butoxide. If that's what you need for your situation, fine, but check the label to avoid surprises.

If you are applying any product that you have never used before, including a new homemade recipe, always test it on a few branches of a plant and wait a day or two before applying it to your entire garden.

ALFALFA AND COTTONSEED MEAL

These are granulated products made from pressed alfalfa hay and the solids remaining after cotton seeds are pressed for oil. They are high in nitrogen and can be added to soil or planting mix as slow-release nitrogen fertilizers.

Look for alfalfa and cottonseed meals at farm animal feed stores and garden centers under many different brands.

AMPELOMYCES QUISQUALIS

Ampelomyces Quisqualis is a hyperparasite that targets a few fungi, but for the purposes of cannabis cultivation, is effective against powdery mildew. It infects mildew colonies, slowing their growth and in some cases eliminates them completely. AQ occurs naturally and is generally endemic to the same places as powdery mildew, minimizing the potential for adverse affects on beneficial organisms. AQ has been extensively tested for agriculture. It has no phytotoxicity and is harmless to humans and beneficial organisms. AQ can be applied on its own but can also be found in several commercially produced organic fungicides.

• AQ10 Bio Fungicide, Fargro

ANT BAITS

These products contain a poison such as boric acid, arsenic or sulfluramid and an attractive bait that entices the ants to carry it back to their nest, where it kills both workers and queens.

Ant baits and ant stakes are very safe methods of dealing with the problem because they use minute amounts of poison in a very targeted way.

The ingredients are not released into the general environment. Instead, the target acquires the slow acting poisons. The affected ants have time to interact with a large number of nest mates so the poison affects a large group. Available in many brands, including Grants Ant Stakes, Terro Liquid Borate Ant Bait, Enforcer Ant Bait, Advance® Dual-Choice Bait Station and Drax Liquidator® Ant Bait Station.

In addition to the direct harm caused to soil condition by tunneling and nesting, ants are notorious for "aphid ranching:" Ants can extract nutrients from aphid excretions and a colony will ferociously protect its aphid "stable" from natural predators. Organic ant baits usually contain Borax, a mineral salt of Boric Acid, which slowly kills ants, allowing time for distribution to the entire colony. It is a natural mineral with minimal toxicity to humans.

- Terro Ant Killer
- Aunt Fannie's Ant Remedy
- Advance Dual Choice Ant Bait Station

APHID MIDGES

Aphidoletes aphidimyza is a small fly (2-3 mm long or .7-.11 in) that looks a little like a mosquito. The larvae are bright orange and are attracted to the smell of honeydew. They attack and consume aphids by the score.

Midge larvae paralyze aphids with an injection of biotoxin to the legs, allowing them to bore a hole in the unfortunate aphid's thorax and suck out the viscera, leaving behind an empty husk. Aphid midges often kill more aphids than they can eat when faced with an especially dense population, making them an excellent control. They're sold as pupae, which can be placed inside a greenhouse or at the center of a field where they will grow into an adult population and lay eggs among the aphids. Using aphid midges in conjunction with parasitic nematodes is not recommended because the nematodes may target pupae.

Buy them as pupae from companies such as Buglogical, Planet Natural, Hydro-Gardens, Natural Insect Control, Peaceful Valley and EcoSolutions. The pupae hatch into adults, which lay eggs and produce the aphid-destroying larvae. Plan on using about 100 pupae per 100 square feet.

- Aphidend
- Arbico

BACILLUS PUMILUS

Bacillus pumilus is a naturally occurring bacterium that produces compounds that kill active fungal infections and inhibit further growth. Strain QST 2808 of this bacterium has been patented for use as a biorational fungicide against Fusarium, gray mold and powdery mildew, under the brand name Sonata®. It is most effective when applied as a preventive measure before symptoms appear.

Sonata® is effective for about 10 days after each application. I found that it does not completely eliminate powdery mildew when used alone, but it does work very well in conjunction with Bacillus subtilis fungicides such as Serenade®.

- Sonata Biofungicide, Bayer

BACILLUS SUBTILIS

Bacillus subtilis is another naturally occurring fungicidal bacterium. Several strains of this bacterium have been patented for use against Fusarium, gray mold, powdery mildew, Pythium and Verticillium under brand names such as Serenade®, Rhizopro® and Subtilex®. It is most effective when applied as a preventive measure before symptoms appear.

Bacillus subtilis colonizes the soil around plant roots and produces antibiotics that suppress the fungi causing root and stem rot. B. subtilis is used as a seed treatment or soil drench. It works better as a preventative, and will not control a serious damping off infestation after it has begun The Bacillus subtilis strain (QST713) is known by the brand name Serenade, is particularly effective against powdery mildew. It uses three chemical pathways to destroy disease causing pathogens. It stops harmful spores from germinating, disrupts growth of the germ tube and mycelia, and inhibits the growth of the fungus at the leaf surface. It is considered totally safe to humans and animals since the bacteria attacks only fungi. Watch out if you are a fungus. Otherwise you are safe. This bacterium is marketed under several names, including Companion and Serenade.

BACILLUS THURINGIENSIS

Bacillus Thuringiensis is a family of bacteria with at least 35 separate strains producing 140 types of spore toxins, the real weapons against pests. Two common BT strains are described here because they contain spore toxins that are active against some common cannabis pests, as well as beetle grubs, fly larvae, and many other soil dwelling insects.

Bacillus thuringiensis (variety israelensis) (Indoors and Outdoors)

FOR FUNGUS GNATS AND MOSQUITOES

This spore toxin exists in the bacteria as a crystalline protein. When a fungus gnat ingests a spore, the protein is dissolved by enzymes in the insect's digestive tract and destroys the cells of the insect's digestive system. Once the spores are ingested, insects stop feeding within an hour. They shrivel, blacken, and die. Bacillus thuringiensis Israelensis does not reproduce in pest populations, so it must be reapplied every week to 10 days. The dust is applied to the surface of the soil or rockwool. Bacillus thuringiensis Israelensis is compatible with some other biocontrol agents, including the beneficial nematode Steinernema sp. and the soil mite Hypoaspis miles. It is marketed as Gnatrol and Bactimos.

FOR CATERPILLARS

Bacillus thuringiensis (var. kurstaki) is one of the best solutions for caterpillars. *Bacillus thuringiensis kurstaki* is a naturally occurring soil bacterium that has been used since the 1930s. It acts selectively, killing caterpillars, but poses no harm to beneficial insects, earthworms, fish, birds, cats, dogs, other mammals, or humans. Bacillus thuringiensis kurstaki renders the caterpillars' stomachs nonfunctional by multiplying inside the digestive tract, creating sharp, toxic, protein crystals.

Bacillus thuringiensis kurstaki does not attack Lepidoptera eggs, but it works well on caterpillars that are chomping on leaves, especially if they are in the earliest stages of caterpillar life. Once the leaves have been sprayed with Bacillus thuringiensis kurstaki, only caterpillars that eat the treated areas will be affected. Bacillus thuringiensis kurstaki affects insects quickly, causing caterpillars to stop eating soon after they've fed on treated plants. Death follows in a day or two. The decaying caterpillar body releases more of the bacteria. Given the lengthy commercial use of this Bacillus thuringiensis strain, there is some concern about caterpillar resistance. There are no known incidences of developed resistance to Bacillus thuringiensis kurstaki among caterpillars. Bacillus thuringiensis kurstaki comes in liquid and wettable powder form. A single application provides permanent protection until it is washed off, so reapply after rain. Bacillus thuringiensis kurstaki breaks down over three to seven days. Since this product works best on young caterpillars, multiple treatments are necessary to eradicate all caterpillars from staggered hatch times. If product instructions call for dilution with water, use non-chlorinated water because chlorine in tap water can destroy the Bacillus thuringiensis kurstaki bacteria, thus rendering the treatment useless. Bacillus thuringiensis kurstaki is widely available in garden stores and through the Internet. Brands include Green Step Caterpillar Control, Dipel Dust, and Bonide BT, Thuricide. Make sure that the ingredient label of any other brand does not list additional chemical pesticides.

BARLEY STRAW RAFTS & PELLETS

Barley straw rafts floating in the water are algaecidal. They are useful in hydroponic systems and reservoirs. This effect is due to hydrogen peroxide produced by a complex series of chemical reactions as the barley decays.

Algae control is a problem for hydroponic growers because it taxes the oxygen resources of the water. Barley straw rafts have been successfully used as an algae control method in large bodies of water like lakes and ponds, however this method is slow and still requires high enough water oxygenation to maintain aerobic decomposition. Barley straw extract can inhibit the growth of algae and is sold as a liquid.

• Barleyclear, NT Labs

BEAUVERIA BASSIANA (BENEFICIAL FUNGI)

Beauveria bassiana is a fungus that attacks and kills a variety of pests, including aphids, caterpillars, leaf miners, spider mites and whiteflies. Note that many beneficial insects, such as lady beetles, are also susceptible. Products containing Beauveria work by contact but take three to seven days to germinate, penetrate and kill target pests. Infected insects stop eating soon after and die in two to 10 days. The fungus' reproductive organs emerge from the corpse as a white mat (hence the name white muscardine disease) and produce spores. B. bassiana does best at 90 percent humidity but works well in the grow room humidity range of 40% - 60 %, with daytime temperatures of 70 to 86 F. Spores do not have to be ingested to work. Spray plants thoroughly as soon as you identify an infestation. In addition to killing off existing pests, it prevents infestation or reinfestation. Spray on all surfaces of infested plants and the medium. Once it establishes in a space, it helps to keep infestations from occurring. Commercial products containing B. bassiana include Naturalis H&G®, Mycotrol® and Botanigard®.

- Mycotrol, Mycothech
- BotaniGard, Mycotech
- Naturalis, Troy BioSciences

BORIC ACID

Boric acid is one of the best cures for boron deficiencies as well as a common, safe and effective ant poison. It is also effective against cockroaches and termites. It can be sprinkled as a powder or laid down as a barrier wherever pests are seen, but it is usually more effective laced into a bait.

The powder sticks to ants' exoskeletons as they walk through a perimeter barrier. When the ants clean themselves, they lick it off, and ingest it. The acid activates as it moistens and it eats the ants' internal organs. Because of its toxicity to ants, it is effective as a food-based pesticide and as a barrier. When ants come in contact with enough of it, it clings to their exoskeletons and desiccates them. Boric acid is safe for bees and birds and it is considered non-hazardous to mammals. Many commercial baits are available, including Drax®, Ant Kil Gel, Borid® and Dr. Moss® Liquid Ant Bait.

You can make your own with these recipes:

Sugar Bait
1 cup sugar
4 teaspoons boric acid

Grease Bait
3 cups water
about 1 cup canned cat food
1 tablespoon boric acid

Mix the ingredients and put small amounts of the solution or cat food mixture in shallow dishes near plants. Keep these baits out of reach of pets and children.

CAL-MAG

These nutrient supplements contain both calcium and magnesium, suitable for correcting deficiencies in either or both of these minerals. Brands include Botanicare® Cal-Mag Plus®, Sensi- Cal®, MagiCal® and Cal-Max®.

Note that different Cal-Mag products contain different levels of nitrogen, phosphorous and potassium, the big three macronutrients. Check the label on the product you're thinking of using, and avoid using high-nitrogen products during flowering or high-phosphorous products during vegetative growth.

Magnesium is a secondary nutrient that plays a crucial role in photosynthesis, making magnesium deficiency a potentially lethal issue for cannabis plants. Calcium is another secondary nutrient, but it is immobile, which means the plant requires a constant supply and cannot draw on stores in older leaves. Formulations of calcium and magnesium are available separately, but many growers prefer Cal-mag products, which when added to your nutrition plan can prevent any deficiencies in the first place.

- Earth Juice, Elements
- Black Magic
- Sensi Cal, Advanced Nutrients
- Botanicare
- MagiCal™, Techanaglora Plant Products LTD

CALCIUM NITRATE

Various compounds such as calcium nitrate ($CaNO_3$) and calcium acetate ($CaCH_3CO_2$) are used to correct calcium deficiencies. Calcium nitrate is especially useful as it provides both calcium and nitrogen in readily available forms. It can be purchased at larger garden centers under the Viking fertilizer brand and through scientific supply houses under brand names such as Aldrich and Sigma.

Beware of using calcium nitrate during the flowering stage because it will provide more nitrogen than the plant should have at that stage of growth.

Calcium nitrate is an inorganic salt that contains high levels of calcium and dissolves easily in water, making it an excellent option for addressing calcium deficiency in cannabis plants. It should not be used during flowering as it will boost the nitrogen levels too high.

- PowerGrow
- Southern Ag

- Greenway Biotech
- YaraLiva

CAPSAICIN

This is the substance that gives hot peppers their heat. Pepper plants produce capsaicin for its repellent value against insects and other animals that might otherwise eat the plants. It provides similar protection when applied to other plants.

Cayenne pepper contains capsaicin, and it can be sprinkled as a powder to repel ants.

- Hot Pepper Wax, Bonide
- Repellex Mole, Vole, and Gopher Repellent
- Browseban™, Repellex®
- Liquid Fence

You can make an insecticidal pepper spray with this recipe:

½ ounce (15 g) dried or 4 ounces (60 g) fresh peppers (habañero or other very hot pepper)
2 tablespoons (30 mL) of vegetable oil
¼ teaspoon (1 g) lecithin granules
¼ teaspoon (1 g) wetting agent
Water to make up one pint (450 ml)

You can also substitute 2 tablespoons (30 mL) of Asian hot pepper oil for peppers. Wear gloves whenever you handle peppers or pepper oil, and avoid touching your eyes or mouth with your gloved hands. Grind the peppers (do not discard the seeds) and oil together in a blender. Add the lecithin granules, wetting agent and water, and mix thoroughly. The mixture can be used immediately but will become stronger if the peppers are allowed to soak. Strain the mixture through cheesecloth or panty hose into a glass jar for storage. Label the jar "Pepper Spray Concentrate." To use, mix 1 or 2 tablespoons (15-30 mL) of this concentrate with 1 pint of water and spray on plants.

As with all home recipes, test this spray on a few leaves and wait a day to check for damage, before applying it to your whole garden.

Commercial products that contain capsaicin include Hot Pepper Spray®, Bonide® Hot Pepper Wax for ants, aphids, leaf miners, spider mites, thrips and whiteflies), Repellex® Mole, Vole and Gopher Repellent (for gophers and moles), Browseban® and Liquid Fence® (for deer).

CARBON DIOXIDE

Plants use carbon dioxide (CO_2) for photosynthesis, and it is present in the atmosphere at 300-400 parts per million (ppm). Growers often use CO_2 tanks to increase the levels of this gas to 1,500-2,000 ppm in their grow rooms and greenhouses. These levels are not harmful to most animal life. However, increasing the carbon dioxide level to 10,000 ppm (1%) and holding it at that level for an hour kills most insects, including aphids, spider mites, thrips and whiteflies. Take care to vent the room thoroughly after this treatment, as such high levels of CO_2 are hazardous for humans as well.

CO_2 is also useful against ants, gophers and moles. Against ants, pour 1 gallon of seltzer water into the anthill, or inject CO_2 into the nest from a tank, using a wand. Against gophers or moles, drop 8 to 16 ounces (225 to 450 grams) of dry ice into the tunnel, or deliver a similar amount of CO_2 from a tank.

Carbon dioxide is crucial for proper plant development, and increasing it will boost plant vigor and resistance to heat. A CO_2 generator is one option for increasing levels, but it will also produce heat, making it impractical for small indoor or greenhouse grows. For a temperature neutral option that allows for slightly more control, compressed CO_2 can be used to release CO_2 from above and fans can be used to circulate it. The atmosphere usually contains around 400ppm or CO_2 and cannabis tends to thrive when that number is between 1,000 and 2,000ppm, but keep in mind that above 3,000ppm CO_2 presents a potentially deadly danger to humans.

- The Enhancer, TBN Naturals
- AG Gas®

CASTOR OIL

This is a popular ingredient in gopher and mole repellents. It repels by both taste and smell. The liquid can be smeared on paper and dropped into the gopher's burrow. Commercial repellents such as Repellex® Mole, Vole and Gopher Repellent,

Molemax® and Sweeney's® Mole & Gopher Repellent may be easier to use.

CHELATED MINERALS

Chelation is a chemical process whereby nutrient minerals (such as boron, copper, iron, magnesium, manganese, zinc and others) are made more available to plants by combining them with a compound such as citric acid or EDTA (ethylenediaminetetraacetic acid). Many hydroponic micronutrient formulas contain a blend of chelated minerals. Other products contain single metal chelates for treating specific deficiencies. Brands depend on the specific mineral of interest:

Copper: LibrelTM Copper Chelate, YEOMAN® 5% Cu

Iron: Bonide Liquid Iron (also contains Zn and Mn), Plant-Prod® Iron Chelate

Manganese: Growth Product Manganese Chelate, LibrelTM Manganese Chelate

Zinc: YEOMAN® 7% Zn, Nulex® Liquid Zinc

Soil conditioners like humic and fulvic acid will encourage chelation in any grow medium.

- Librel Copper Chelate, Cooper
- Liquid Iron, Bonide
- Manganese Chelate, Growth Products
- Liquid Zinc, Nulex®

CHOLECALCIFEROL (VITAMIN D$_3$)

This is one of the more modern rat poisons, developed because it is significantly less toxic to humans than it is to rats and mice. Of course all rat poisons should be treated with care and deployed only in tamper-proof bait stations. Commercial baits such as Quintox® and Campaign® are effective.

This form of Vitamin D is lethal to rats and mice that are resistant to anti-coagulants. It's a one time feeding bait that kills rodents through hypercalcemia, leaving minimal secondary toxicity in their tissues because of its rapid efficacy. It had a low toxicity to birds.

- Terad 3 pellets,
- Selontra, BASF

CINNAMON OIL AND TEA

Cinnamon destroys powdery mildew, with an effectiveness rate of 50-70%. It doesn't eradicate mildew completely, but it keeps the mildew in check. It also potentiates other suppressive sprays so it is good to use cinnamon and sprays in combination with other methods of control. In addition to its fungicidal properties, cinnamon is effective against ants, aphids, fungus gnats, spider mites, thrips and whiteflies.

Mix food grade oil (available at herb shops and natural food stores) at the rate of 1 part to 200 parts water or a bit under 1 teaspoon (5 mL) per quart (950 mL). Or make a tea directly from cinnamon: boil water, turn off the heat and let cool for a few minutes, then add 1 ounce of cinnamon to 1½ pints water. Let the tea cool to room temperature. Add half a pint of 100 proof grain alcohol or rubbing alcohol and let sit. Strain the cinnamon. The spray is ready to use. A faster method is to add 2 teaspoons (10 mL) cinnamon oil to 1 pint (500 mL) of water and add a dash of castile soap. Rosemary oil and thyme oil are also sometimes combined with cinnamon oil. The solution should consist of no more than 0.75% total oil.

Repel ants with cinnamon powder, either alone or mixed 50/50 with diatomaceous earth. Sprinkle the powder wherever you find ants entering.

Ed Rosenthal's Zero Tolerance® contains cinnamon oil in both its pesticide and fungicide formulations. Dr. Earth® Pro-Active™ Fruit and Vegetable Insect Spray, Cinnacure® and FlowerPharm™ are other brand-name preparations.

CITRIC ACID

- The Amazing Dr. Zymes
- Plant Therapy

CLOVE OIL

Clove oil is used in some botanical fungicides. Eugenol, a component of clove oil, is both a fungicide and a potent contact insecticide. It has virtually no residual activity, although the scent lingers. Eugenol is considered a minimum risk ingredient of pesticides. It has very low risk of damage to the environment or user. It is effective against ants, aphids, caterpillars, Fusarium, gray mold, Pythium, spider mites and thrips.

Ed Rosenthal's Zero Tolerance® contains clove oil in both its pesticide and fungicide formulations. Dr. Earth® Pro-Active™ Fruit and Vegetable Insect Spray, Phyta-Guard EC, GC-Mite®, Natura Bug-A-Tak® and Bioganic® Lawn and Garden Spray are also commercial clove oil preparations.

- Ed Rosenthal's Zero Tolerance Pesticide by Natural Garden Solutions

COMPOST & COMPOST TEA

Compost is rich black material similar to soil, produced by the controlled decomposition of organic materials (vegetable scraps, yard waste, etc.). You can buy it at garden centers, or make your own. It is a rich source of beneficial microbes and micronutrients and provides many benefits to improve overall plant health. The beneficial microbes in compost act as barriers to infection and also destroy pathogenic organisms.

It can be worked into the soil or incorporated into a container planting mix before planting, and it can be prepared as a tea and applied by irrigation or foliar spray. Compost tea requires special care in hydroponic systems. It presents no difficulties as a foliar spray, but it should be added to the nutrient solution only in drip-to-drain systems and should be thoroughly filtered before use.

Some hydroponic shops prepare compost tea on the premises and sell it fresh. They also sell kits under brands such as SoilSoup and Vermicorp to enable home users to make their own. To prepare your own tea, you can use one of these kits, or assemble a bucket, an aquarium air pump (with hose and "bubbler" attached), a nylon stocking and enough compost to fill the bucket about one-quarter full. Buckets larger than 1 gallon (4 L) may require more bubblers for adequate aeration.

Load the compost into the stocking to make a "compost teabag." Tie the end of the stocking to the bucket handle and put the bag in the bucket. Some compost tea recipes call for molasses. However, this encourages the growth of E. coli and other pathogenic bacteria. Fill the bucket with water and put the air hose and bubbler from the pump at the bottom of the bucket. Run the bubbler to keep the solution aerated for about a day. Switch off the pump and let the tea settle. The liquid in the bucket should be deep brown, with no unpleasant smell. A smell of ammonia or rot means that the tea has become anaerobic and should not be used as a foliar spray.

Compost tea must be used as quickly as possible because it turns anaerobic within a few hours after aeration stops. Strain the liquid through a cheesecloth strainer or filter and apply as a foliar spray or add it to your irrigation water. The used compost can be spread on the surface of the soil around the plants.

Compost and compost tea are "tonics" that promote plant health and help to prevent disease, not specific cures for any pathogen. The effectiveness of these preparations depends greatly on how they're made, but well-made compost can do a lot to produce healthy plants.

COPPER

Copper has been used as a fungicide for centuries. However, ingestion of copper is hazardous to humans and pets, and it is not permitted in some states. Spraying it can lead to ingestion, which has health consequences. Don't use this substance Copper fungicides are implicated in toxicological problems of farm workers who are in contact with them. Cannabis treated with copper is inhale or ingest.

Copper has numerous applications for agriculture, but its most common use for cannabis is the creation of a Bordeaux Mixture, which is comprised of equal parts copper sulfate and calcium oxide from slaked lime and used as a fungicide.

COPPER STRIPPING (OUTDOORS)
FOR SLUGS AND SNAILS
A 2- to 4-inch-wide circular strip of copper reacts chemically with the slug or snail's slime and repels them with a small electric shock. Use a copper screen, flashing, or strips around the plant or the garden perimeter. Keep the surface of the copper clean for the best reactions. These bands are available commercially for use around the base of pots or around the base of single-stem plants. They are sold under a variety of commercial names but are generally known as "slug rings."

CORIANDER OIL

This natural essential oil acts as a fungicide and insecticide to control aphids, Fusarium, gray mold, powdery mildew, Pythium, Septoria, spider mites, thrips and whiteflies. It can be purchased in a commercial blend with canola oil and a pH buffer as SM-90®.

Copper has numerous applications for agriculture, but its most common use for cannabis is the creation of a Bordeaux Mixture, which is comprised of equal parts copper sulfate and calcium oxide from slaked lime and used as a fungicide.

COTTONSEED MEAL

When cotton is processed the seeds are separated from the fiber and used to produce cottonseed oil, which entails mechanically separating the seeds from their hulls and extracting the oil using solvents or pressing. The kernel meat remaining after extraction is called cottonseed meal and it can be used as an organic fertilizer. The exact levels will vary somewhat, but the N-P-K ratio of cottonseed meal is roughly 7-3-2.

CULTURAL CONTROLS

This category doesn't refer to social customs but rather to ways of cultivating plants that help minimize or eliminate pests. For example, allowing the soil around plants to dry somewhat between waterings helps to control many sorts of soil-borne fungi and also reduces the population of fungus gnats. Watering in the mornings allows the soil to dry out before slugs and snails come out at night.

Growing in containers with pasteurized planting mix (either indoors or out) reduces or eliminates many soil-dwelling fungi and pests.

In outdoor gardens, maintain a favorable environment for beneficial insects and they'll do a lot of your pest control for you. Indoors, keep grow room humidity under 50% to help prevent gray mold.

Keep light out of hydroponic water systems to prevent growth of algae. Keep your grow room clean and never bring in clothing that has just been outdoors—this helps keep out many pests.

Cultural controls are a key feature of IPM and encompass all the non-chemical crop management practices used to control pests and other plant ailments. Crop rotation, companion planting, thorough sanitation of the grow and surrounding areas are examples.

CREAM OF TARTAR

This material is available at most grocery stores. In addition to its many cooking uses, it repels ants. To apply cream of tartar, first determine where the ants are entering. This usually means following an ant trail back to a crack or other small opening in a wall, baseboard or window. Once the point of entry is found, sprinkle a liberal coating of cream of tartar on and around the opening.

D-LIMONENE (INDOORS AND OUTDOORS)
For molds and fungi, ants, aphids, fungus gnats, mites, root aphids, scales, thrips, and whiteflies

D-limonene is an essential oil from the rinds of citrus fruits including oranges, lemons, and limes. It smells like citrus. It is the active ingredient in citrus-scented cleaning products. D-limonene's mode of action is similar to pyrethrum. It both repels and paralyzes insects. It is available in a variety of formulations to kill and repel ants, hornets, wasps, fleas, and other insects. It is harmful to beneficial insects if sprayed directly on them. It also controls molds and fungi including Pythium, Fusarium and Rhizoctonia. Commercial products include Ortho Home Defense Indoor Insect Killer, Clean Green All Purpose Cleaner, TKO, D'Bug Safer Brand Ant and Roach Killer, Surefire Crawling Insect Killer, and Orange Guard Fire Ant Control.

DIATOMACEOUS EARTH

Diatoms are microscopic sea creatures with hard silica shells. The diatoms of ancient seas left large deposits of a chalky mineral that can be easily crumbled into a white powder: diatomaceous earth. This is available at most garden supply shops. Their fossilized remains are a brittle, white talc-like powder that can be used as either a soil conditioner or a pesticide. It is harmless to humans and is often found in grain, which it is stored with to prevent pests.

Diatomaceous earth contains microscopic fragments of glassy silica that injure and even kill small, soft-bodied animals. Kill fungus gnat larvae and thrips pupae by placing a layer about 1 inch (2.5 cm) deep atop the soil in plant pots. Deter ants, slugs and snails with a thin but unbroken barrier of diatomaceous earth about 3 inches (7 to 8 cm) wide. Mix with boric acid, ground cinnamon or ground cloves to increase its effectiveness. It becomes ineffective when it is wet because the spikes soften.

FERTILIZERS

Basic garden fertilizers are rated by their NPK numbers. These are noted on the label as a series of three numbers such as 15-5-10, 5-1-1, etc., describing the content of the three major macronutrients in the product. The first number always represents the nitrogen (N) content of the fertilizer. The number is the percent of the element in the fertilizer. The second represents the equivalent of the phosphorous compound P2O5. The third is the equivalent of the potassium (K) compound K2O (potash). Thus, a fertilizer with NPK values of 10-5-1 would contain 10% nitrogen, 5% equivalent of P2O5 phosphate and 1% equivalent of the potassium compound potash. For brevity's sake, they are called N-P-K.

Choose a fertilizer according to the deficiency (if any) that you are trying to treat, and also to the growth stage of the plants. Nitrogen promotes vegetative growth, so it is most needed during the vegetative period. Avoid fertilizers high in nitrogen during the flowering stage. Conversely, phosphorous is most needed during flowering and should be used with care during vegetative growth. Potassium is useful at all stages of a plant's growth and is added to balance the pH of high-phosphorous fertilizers.

Proper plant nutrition is crucial to maintaining general health. Make sure you factor in the N-P-K ratio of any potential fertilizer or additive and keep an eye out for impacts on pH balance.

- Sierra Naturals Perfect Mix 3 part System
- Reiziger Grow Food A &B
- Reiziger Grow Booster
- Organics Solutions Premium Worm Castings
- Organics Solutions Superchar

FISH EMULSION AND FISH MEAL

Whole fish deemed unsuitable for regular food use (such as menhaden), and the bones and offal from processed fish, are pressed to remove the fish oil. The remains after this pressing are a brown powder (fish meal) and a liquid emulsion (fish emulsion). Both are high in nitrogen and useful organic fertilizers (especially for treating nitrogen deficiencies). They also provide many micronutrients that help prevent deficiencies.

Fish emulsion releases nitrogen to the plant more rapidly, whereas fish meal provides a steady, slow release. Look for brands such as Alaska Fish Emulsion, Fertrell Liquid Fish Emulsion, Down To Earth Fish Meal and Peaceful Valley Fish Meal.

FUMIGANTS

Sometimes the only way to eliminate gophers and moles is by gassing them. Several "smoke bombs" are sold for this purpose, such as Dexol Gopher Gasser and Revenge Rodent Smoke Bomb. These are thick paper cartridges filled with charcoal, sodium nitrate and sometimes sulfur. You light the fuse and put it in the gopher's burrow. Toxic fumes from the burning cartridge do the rest.

Fumigation usually involves the use of toxic chemicals, but organic fumigation is possible using carbon dioxide. This is often done in sealed environments, like grain or fruit silos, because it leaves no toxic residue on or in the food. However, it can be difficult and dangerous to maintain the required CO_2 levels long enough to kill both the insects and their offspring.

FUNGICIDES

- ZeroTol 2.0, Biosafe Systems
- ZeroTol HC , Biosafe Systems
- Dr. Zymes
- Vitaloxide , Ecology Works
- Lost Coast Plant Therapy
- Ed Rosenthal's Zero Tolerance Fungicide

GARLIC

Garlic is antifungal and antibacterial. It is used as an ingredient in fungicides and can be prepared as a spray and used every few days. Garlic has several pathways for destroying fungi, including its high sulfur content. Garlic can also be added to other antifungal sprays.

You can make your own garlic spray from a teaspoon of garlic oil in a pint of water with 2 ounces (60 mL) of 100 proof or higher drinking alcohol such as rum or vodka. Use garlic as a preventive. Spray on new growth before there is a sign of infection.

Apply about every 10 days. The odor lingers so it should not be used for two weeks before harvesting. Garlic spray is rinsed from the leaves by rain so it should be reapplied when the storm has passed.

Garlic is a general-purpose insecticide as well as fungicide, so it should be used with caution on outdoor plants. Garlic insecticides kill beneficial insects as well as plant pests like ants, aphids, caterpillars, spider mites, thrips and white-flies. Brands include Dr. Earth Pro-Active™ Fruit and Vegetable Insect Spray, VeggiePharm®, Garlic Barrier®, BioRepel® and Envirepel®.

Garlic is also an ingredient in several commercial deer repellents, such as Deer-Off® and DeerPharm®.

GLIOCLADIUM (BENEFICIAL FUNGUS)

Gliocladium is a genus of soil-dwelling fungi that attack and destroy pathogenic fungi such as Fusarium and Pythium. It is best applied as a soil drench before any symptoms of infection are noticed. *Gliocladium* fungicides are sold under brands such as Glio-mix®, SoilGard®, Primastop® and Prestop®.

GRAPEFRUIT SEED EXTRACT

Grapefruit seed extract is sold as a general-purpose disinfectant and can be used to control algae in hydroponic systems. Look for brands such as Citricidal® and Nutribiotic®. Follow label instructions for control of algae, as different brands contain different concentrations of grapefruit seed extract.

GRANITE DUST

The powdered rock left over from quarrying granite (called rock dust, granite dust or stone meal) is a good slow-release source of potassium in soil and container gardening. Depending on the source of the stone, granite dust may also contain a variety of micronutrients, which are listed on the label. It is available through garden shops under brand names including Fishers Creek, Down To Earth and Agrowinn.

Granite dust is made by pulverizing naturally occurring granite stones. The resulting powder is an excellent soil amendment that will provide a steady source of minerals like calcium and will also supplement iron and manganese.

GREENSAND

Greensand is not really sand but rather a soft, easily crumbled form of sandstone rock that is usually colored dark green. The green color comes from an iron-potassium silicate mineral called glauconite. As you might expect, greensand is a good slow-release source of potassium and iron when you don't want to introduce nitrogen as well. Greensand is also a significant source of phosphorous and contains small amounts of many other micronutrients such as copper and manganese. Brands include Fertrell® Jersey Greensand, Gardener's Supply Company Greensand and various local and store brands.

A naturally occurring sandstone, Greensand contains high levels of iron and potassium because of the presence of glauconite. It is an excellent soil amendment for organic gardening because of its mineral properties, as well as its ability to absorb water in soils with high levels of clay and retain it in sandy soils.

GUANO

The droppings (guano) of bats and seabirds are harvested commercially and sold as organic fertilizers. Depending on the source, guano is high in nitrogen, phosphorous or both, and is an excellent relatively available fertilizer for treating or preventing deficiencies in these nutrients. Because guano varies widely, always check the NPK value on the label to make sure that a given guano fertilizer meets your needs. Guano is available under many different brands through garden supply shops.

To make the nutrients in guano more readily available to the plants, simmer the guano in water in a slow cooker outside, to avoid a major odor problem. Most of the nutrients will dissolve into the water and will then be available for immediate uptake by the plants. If you are making a large quantity, you may wish to prepare a concentrate to be diluted later. Keep refrigerated. The solution can be used either as a foliar spray or for irrigation.

GYPSUM

Gypsum is a natural mineral composed of calcium sulfate ($CaSO_4$). It is useful as a slow-release form of calcium or sulfur that doesn't affect the soil pH too much. It should not be added to soils with a pH below 5.5 because it interacts with aluminum (Al) in those acidic soils, making the Al soluble and poisonous to the plants. Gypsum is available at garden centers under various local and store brands.

Gypsum can also be used to break up clay soils and is a naturally occurring mineral which, like lime, is high in calcium and can be used to address deficiencies.

Herbal & Essential Oils
Ants, aphids, caterpillars, fungus gnats, gray mold, mealybugs, powdery mildew, scales, spider mites, thrips, and whiteflies

Herbal oils are made from a range of plants, including cinnamon, citronella, clove, coriander, eucalyptus, lavender, lemongrass, mint, oregano, rosemary, and thyme. They can be used close to harvest because they evaporate in five to 10 days and do not leave a residue. These oils are some of Mother Nature's repellents, and contact insecticides and fungicides that deteriorate the bodies of insects and mites as well as kill molds and fungi. When developing my herbal oil products, oils from plants that were not bothered by mites, ants, aphids, and powdery mildew were selected. By blending together several oils, there is a multi-prong attack: Some oils deteriorate the exoskeleton of the pest, while others destroy the internal tissue, and others the nervous system. Multiple applications of herbal oils break up the life cycle of the pest.

For spider mites spraying three times, three to four days apart, will eliminate them by knocking out hatchlings. Mist plants late in the day or late in the light cycle for indoor gardens. Always spray directly on pests that often reside on the underside of leaves. Store herbal oils in a cool, dark place with the cap firmly sealed. Availability of commercial pesticides and fungicides based on herbal oils has increased. Ed Rosenthal's Zero Tolerance will eliminate mites as well as a wide range of soft-bodied insects and mold diseases Dr. DoRight's blends oils as a defense against powdery mildew. Miticides include SNS-217 Spider Mite Control and Rasta Bob's Death Mite. If the pests are in the soil, use a soil drench product like SNS-203.

- Ed Rosenthal's Zero Tolerance
- Plant Therapy

HORTICULTURAL OIL

Horticultural oils are any of a number of light oils used to control insects such as aphids, fungus gnats, leaf miners, mealybugs, scales, spider mites, thrips and whiteflies. They work by smothering insects, and so they must be applied directly to the target pests. They provide no residual activity. Some horticultural oils are vegetable-based, while others are petroleum-based. Both are effective, but if you wish to avoid petroleum products, be sure to check the label. In any case, petroleum-based oils should not be used on buds, or on leaves that you plan to use for cooking, collecting kief, or making extracts.

These oils need to be distinguished from neem oil, which poisons pests, although, like neem oil, some horticultural oils such as cottonseed oil, jojoba and sesame have fungicidal properties. They can be used in combination with other spray ingredients listed here. The oils are mixed at about 1-2% concentrations. A 1% solution is about 1 teaspoon per pint (5 mL per 500 mL), 3 tablespoons per gallon (40 mL per 4 L) and 1 quart in 25 gallons. Add a wetting agent or castile soap to help the ingredients mix.

Oil sprays should be used only on the leaves, not the buds. Use weekly on new growth. Horticultural oils are classified as "dormant" oils, which are used on plants during the winter season, and "summer" oils, which are used on growing plants. Summer oils tend to be lighter and more highly refined. Some oils can be used for either purpose. Marijuana gardens need only summer oils, and dormant oils can harm growing plants. So check the label on any horticultural oil you're thinking of using in your garden to verify that it is rated for use on growing plants. Some suitable brands include Dr. Earth Pro-Active™ Fruit and Vegetable Insect Spray, GC-Mite®, Organocide™, Control Solutions Ultra Fine Oil and Green Light Horticultural Oil.

- Monterey Horticultural Oil
- JMS Stylet Oil

HYDROGEN PEROXIDE

Hydrogen peroxide HP, chemical formula H_2O_2) is a contact disinfectant that leaves no residue. Use it to control algae, gray mold, Pythium and powdery mildew, fungus gnats and spider mites.. Hp can be used daily with no adverse effects on the plants: it produces only oxygen and water vapor as it works.

Household hp sold in drugstores has a concentration of 3%. Garden shops sell 10% hp. ZeroTol® contains 27% hydrogen dioxide and 5% peroxyacetic acid, with an activity equivalent to about 40% hp. It is considered hazardous because it can cause skin burn similar to that caused by concentrated acids.

HP is a great prophylactic treatment because it kills any spores and organisms with which it comes in contact, whether on table and wall surfaces, or on the plants themselves. It is used to sterilize equipment and spaces and can be used in combination with other treatments.

To treat plants with drugstore grade 3% hp, use 4½ tablespoons (70 mL) and fill to make a pint (500 mL) of solution, or a quart of hp to 3 quarts of water.

With horticultural grade 10% hp, use about 4 teaspoons per pint (20 mL per 500 mL) and 10 ounces per gallon (300 mL per 4 liters).

With ZeroTol use about 2 teaspoons per pint (10 mL per 500 mL) and 5 tablespoons per gallon (75 mL per 4 liters).

HYDROPONIC MICRONUTRIENT PRODUCTS

Hydroponic supply companies stock a variety of products that are intended to supply the many micronutrients (as opposed to nitrogen, phosphorous and potassium, the macronutrients) that plants need. They are useful for treating or preventing various micronutrient deficiencies, including copper, molybdenum and iron deficiencies. Brands include BetterGrowHydro Micro-Mix, General Hydroponics FloraMicro and Bio-Genesis® Mineral Matrix Micro-Nutrient Supplement.

Note that some micronutrient products contain macronutrient fertilizers as well. There's nothing inherently wrong with that, as long as you use a product that is balanced to provide the appropriate levels of nitrogen, phosphorous and potassium for the plants' current stage of growth. Likewise, if you're trying to treat a specific micronutrient deficiency, you'll want to be sure that the product you're using contains that nutrient. Always check the labels on nutrient products to make sure you know what you're getting.

IRON PHOSPHATE (FERRIC PHOSPHATE)

Iron phosphate is one of the best organic means of eliminating slugs and snails. Once they eat a small amount of iron phosphate, the pests stop feeding and soon die. It is harmless to plants and pets, unlike poisons such as metaldehyde. Iron phosphate comes in small white pellets. Sprinkle it liberally in a perimeter pattern around your garden, as well as in shrubbery, ground cover and other places where slugs and snails like to hide during the day. Sprinkle it over larger areas and across snail/slug paths. It is safe for humans and pets. Brands include Slug-go® and Escar-go®.

IRON SUPPLEMENTS

Use these products to correct iron deficiencies. Most contain chelated iron, iron sulfate or iron oxides. Brands include Glorious Gardens™ Iron Sulfate, Bonide® Iron Sulfate, Monterey Dr. Iron, Phyto-Plus® Iron 5% and Biomin® Iron.

- Liquid Seaweed (2% iron), Maxicrop/Arbico
- ChaChing, Fox Farm
- CalMax, Grotek

KELP CONCENTRATES

Kelp is a family of seaweeds. Certain types can be harvested and prepared as liquid or granular plant supplements. These concentrates contain a wide range of vitamins, minerals and macro- and micronutrients. They are especially useful for treating potassium and copper deficiencies. Brands include Kelp Help Liquid Kelp Concentrate, Gardens Alive® Liquid Kelp Spray, Bonide® Organic Sea-Green® Kelp Extract Concentrate and Tidal Organics Kelp Meal.

- Age Old® Kelp by Age Old Nutrients

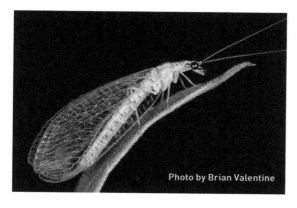

Photo by Brian Valentine

LACEWING

The green lacewing is a very useful beneficial insect. It takes its name from the adult stage, which looks like a small, green fly with fine lacy wings. The larval stage looks something like a grub or caterpillar, with an alligator-like mouth that makes it easy to distinguish from plant eaters. Both the adult and larval stages are ferocious predators of aphids, small caterpillars, whiteflies and any other small insects they can catch.

The main drawback to lacewings is that you can't use them with other beneficial insects: the lacewings and their larvae are such fierce predators that they will eat other beneficials, or even each other if food is scarce.

Use lacewings in greenhouses and outdoor gardens but not in grow rooms.

Outdoors, the adults will tend to fly away once they emerge from the larval stage.

Main species of interest are *Chrysopa rufilabris* and *Chrysopa carnea*. Buy them as either larvae or eggs from companies such as Bio Ag, Gardens Alive, Rincon-Vitova, Planet Natural, Natural Insect Control and American Insectaries. Plan on using about 1,000 eggs or 200 larvae for every 100 square feet (9 square meters).

- Green Lacewing Eggs (*C. rufilabris*), Arbico
- Chrysopa, (*C. Carnea* eggs)

LADY BEETLES

Photo by Mark Plonsky

As cute as lady beetles may be, both the adults and larvae are voracious pest predators. Like lacewings, lady beetles are also best suited to greenhouse and outdoor gardens. They tend to make suicide dives at the hot lights, so you'll end up with dead insects all over your grow space. Though if you buy them as adults, they're even more likely to fly away outdoors.

Choose the species depending on your pest. *Hippodamia convergens* attacks aphids, while *Cryptolaemus montrouzieri* and *Ryzobius lophanthae* devour mealybugs and scale. Buy them as adults or larvae from companies such as Bio Ag, Gardens Alive, Rincon-Vitova, Planet Natural, The Ladybug Company, Ladybug Farms and EcoSolutions. Plan on using about 150 adults or larvae for every 100 square feet (9 square meters).

H. convergens, the common Lady beetle, lays eggs are cream or yellow in color and about one millimeter long. The eggs are laid in clusters on leaves, near prey. The number of eggs laid and their fertility depends on food abundance, ranging from 20 to 1000. When they hatch, the newborns are less than 1 millimeter in length. They immediately search for food. The mothers lay infertile eggs for the hatchlings to eat as their first food. The larvae look a lot like crocodiles. They molt three times into four instars, growing to 1 centimeter in a month. Then they spin a cocoon attached to a leaf and pupate for three days to two weeks depending on species and temperature. The pupae are often brightly colored yellow and orange. Newly emerged adults look for food and sex.

- Arbico Organics

LIGHTING

- BRe³ WAND, Bioradience
- Liquid Cooled LED, GS Thermal Solutions

LIME

Lime is a general term for several calcium or calcium-magnesium compounds. All are highly alkaline and can be used to adjust soil pH upward or to correct calcium and magnesium deficiencies. All of these release calcium/magnesium slowly into the soil.

Calcitic lime will provide only calcium, but the use of dolomitic lime will also provide a magnesium boost. Lime also helps remediate acidic soil by introducing carbonates.

All forms of lime suitable for gardening can be found in large garden centers and through online garden supply shops. These different varieties of lime include:

- **Hydrated lime:** Also called slaked lime, this is calcium hydroxide $(Ca[OH]_2)$. It is the most alkaline form of lime suitable for gardening, so only small amounts are needed to adjust soil pH. It is widely available, usually under various local or store brands.
- **Garden lime:** Garden lime is crushed limestone or oyster shells. The main component is calcium carbonate $(CaCO_3)$, the same form of calcium found in ordinary eggshells. It is less strongly alkaline than hydrated lime, but it still raises soil pH. Brands include Planet Natural Oyster Shell Lime and Espoma® Organic Traditions™ Garden Lime.
- **Dolomitic lime:** A lime that contains dolomite, a mineral high in magnesium. This makes it useful for treating magnesium as well as calcium deficiencies. Brands include Speedi-Grow® - Agricultural Lime and Espoma® Organic Traditions™ Dolomitic Lime and many others.
- **Liquid lime:** Liquid lime products are very finely ground gar-den lime or dolomitic lime in a liquid suspension. Because the particles are so finely divided, they raise soil pH more quickly than regular powdered limes do. Brands include Turbo Turf Liquid Lime Plus®, Aggrene Natural Liquid Lime® and Aggrand Organic Liquid Lime®.

MAGNESIUM SULFATE

Magnesium sulfate ($MgSO_4$) is one of the fastest methods of correcting magnesium and sulfur deficiencies. Apply a solution of 1 teaspoon of Epsom salts per gallon of water (5 mL per 4 liters) in hydroponic reservoirs or as a foliar spray to treat deficiencies and in planting mixes. After the first treatment, treat with one-quarter dose with each watering or change of reservoir. It is sold in most large drugstores as Epsom salts.

MECHANICAL CONTROLS

Many pests can be effectively controlled by physically removing and destroying them. Often these methods can prevent or eliminate minor infestations, and they supplement other controls in more severe infestations. Some of the more common methods include:

Air filtration: Fungal spores and small insect pests such as aphids, spider mites and whiteflies can enter a grow space through the air intake. A fine dust filter keeps these pests out.

Boiling water: Pour boiling water into anthills to destroy these pests. Do not use this method within about 3 feet (1 m) of the plants, however, as it may damage their roots. Add ground cinnamon or clove to improve efficacy.

Bug zappers: Flying insects such as egg-laying moths are attracted to the blue light and electrocuted on the charged grid.

Handpicking and Shaking: Slugs, snails, caterpillars and similar large pests can be picked off the plants by hand whenever they're spotted. Crush them or drop them in a bucket of soapy water to drown them. Look for snails and slugs in the early morning hours, as they hide from light during the day. Shake them off the plants.

Physical barriers: Water moats prevent ants from crossing. For example, put plant containers on blocks in a wide pan and fill the pan with water. Use old vegetable cans as cutworm barriers at the bases of plants. Wrap plants in steel wool to discourage rats. Use copper tape or wire to keep out slugs and snails.

Vacuuming: An ordinary vacuum cleaner can help control ants, aphids, caterpillars, spider mites (and their webs) and whiteflies. Use the vacuum hose and brush attachment, or a handheld vacuum cleaner such as a Dustbuster, to suck them out of the plants. Don't get the hose close enough to suck leaves or buds in, as this may damage them.

Water spray: Remove and drown aphids, mites, ants and caterpillars by knocking them off the plants with a strong stream of water from a hose.

Wiping: Remove mealybugs and scale using a cotton swab moistened with rubbing alcohol.

- Arbico Yellow Pest Insect Traps

MILK

Milk kills powdery mildew so well that rose growers all over the world have adopted it for their fungicidal sprays. It is used by home gardeners and commercial growers for many other crops as well. Use 1 part milk to 9 parts water. I've used only 1% milk, but some recipes call for either whole or skim milk and use up to 1 part in 5 milk. Some recipes add garlic or cinnamon to the mix. When using more than 30% milk, a benign mold is reported to grow on top of the leaves. This mold is harmless to the plant but not good for smokers, so if you notice such growth after using a milk spray, just reduce the concentration of milk in subsequent sprays.

To enhance effectiveness add 1 teaspoon potassium bicarbonate to the mix.

Use a milk spray at the first sign of infection. Then protect the new growth weekly.

Photo by Tom Murray

MINUTE PIRATE BUGS

The minute pirate bug (Orius sp.) is small, only ⅛ to 1/10 of an inch (1.5 millimeters) long, so it picks appropriately sized victims. Thrips and spider mites are its preferred food, but it also enjoys sucking the sweet flesh of small aphids, insect eggs, an occasional caterpillar, or anything else it can catch. Once the thrips population is under control, pirate bugs survive on aphids, mites, scales, whiteflies, and other biological controls, and each other. The minute pirate bug is a true bug: Its mouth is modified into a sharp hollow beak through which it slurps its dinner. The bug catches its prey, holds it with its two front legs, and uses its beak to pierce the exoskeleton. Then it sucks the victim's flesh through its built-in straw Buy them as adults from companies such as Planet

Natural, Rincon-Vitova, Bioplanet and Natural Insect Control. Plan on using about 50 adults for every 100 square feet (9 square meters).

MYCORRHIZAE

Mycorrhizae literally means "fungus-roots" and defines the beneficial symbiotic relationship between specialized soil fungi (*Mycorrhizal* fungi) and plant roots. A garden of microbes grows along a plant's root surfaces. *Mycorrhizal* fungi extract nutrients and transport them to the root. There are two types of these beneficial soil fungi: *endomycorrhizae* actually penetrate the plant's root cells, while *ectomycorrhiza* form sheaths at the root tip.

Mycorrhizal inoculants are best applied at the beginning of the season. The goal is to establish and maintain a healthy colony. Once established, the colony should be self-perpetuation

Plants with mycorrhizal roots are better fed, more drought resistant, and have a higher resistance to pathogenic infections. Another benefit provided is the filling of their environmental niche in the ecosystem, taking resources that otherwise may be available to pathogenic fungi. The fungi attach to the plant's roots, feeding on the plant's carbohydrates. In return, the fungi supply the plant with moisture, nitrogen, phosphorus, copper, calcium, magnesium, zinc, and iron, which the fungus collects and makes available to the plant.

Custom-blended mycorrhizal mixes can be added to your soil to encourage healthy root growth. Mycorrhizal products include MycoApply®, Rooters™ Mycorrhizae Super Pack, Plant Success™, MycoGrow™ and SoilMoist™, among others. Benefits include:

- Improved nutrient and water uptake
- Improved root growth
- Improved plant growth and yield
- Reduced transplant shock
- Reduced drought stress

Products available are:

- Sohum Living Soils Root Probiotic
- Great White, Plant Revolution
- Voodoo Juice, Advanced Nutrients
- Groundwork BioAg

NEEM OIL

Neem oil is pressed from the seed of the neem tree (Azadirachta indica), native to Southeast Asia but now cultivated worldwide. It is an effective killer of ants, aphids, fungus gnats, gray mold, leaf miners, mealybugs, powdery mildew, scale, Septoria, thrips and whiteflies. The crude oil has both insecticidal and fungicidal properties and contains at least 70 components. One group of these is the azadirachtins, which are said to account for 90% of the oil's insecticidal activity. Other compounds including meliantriol, nimbin, nimbidin and salannin also have fungicidal qualities. Neem oil has low mammalian toxicity. In fact it is sometimes used as a toothpaste ingredient in India, and neem twigs are chewed and used as toothbrushes. It degrades rapidly once it is applied so it is safe for the environment, including nontarget species and beneficial insects.

Neem oil protects plants from fungus in several ways. First, it has fungicidal properties on contact as it disrupts the organism's metabolism. Second, it forms a barrier between the plant and the invading fungus. Third, it inhibits spore germination. It has translinear action, that is, it is absorbed by the leaf and moves around using the leaf's circulatory system. It can also be used as a systemic. Neem oil products are effective as foliar sprays and may also be added to soil or grow media in the irrigation water (1 teaspoon neem oil per quart, or 5 mL per liter). When applied in this way, neem products are taken up by the plant's roots and distributed throughout the plant. As a foliar spray, neem oil should be diluted with water and a dash of wetting agent to a 1-2% solution. This solution should be used within eight hours. The fungicidal and insecticidal effects are more potent when applied by spray, but the systemic neem lasts longer. For fungicidal applications, neem oil is best used before the plant or the garden exhibits a major infection. Used in this way, it prevents the spores from germinating.

A few brands use cold-pressed or steam-pressed extract of the neem seed. These contain all of the oils found in the seed. Brands include Dyna-Gro, Monterey, Southern Organix, and United Industries.

Azadirachtin and some other components can be removed from the oil with alcohol. The oil that remains after this treatment is called Clarified Hydrophobic Extract of Neem Oil. This gives three main classes of neem garden products:

- Those with azadirachtin act as broad-spectrum insecticides. Brands include Agroneem, Azatrol, Bioneem and Neemix.
- Those that contain hydrophobic extract of neem oil are both fungicidal and insecticidal but less effective as insecticides than those based on azadirach-

tin. Brands include Trilogy, Tri-act and Green Light Fruit, Nut & Vegetable Spray.

- Those that contain both azadirachtin and extract of neem oil, or pure pressed and filtered neem oil, are more effective as insecticides than either alone. Brands include Azatin-Plus, Dyna-gro™ and Ecoside.

Water soluble neem products are also available. Neem cake remains after all of the oil has been extracted from the seed. It still contains insecticidal, nematicidal, and fungicidal properties, and high percentages of N-P-K and micronutrients. In India it is used as a fertilizer. It is applied at the rate of about an ounce per square foot, applied either as a mulch or mixed into the soil

Neem oil should not be applied for three weeks before harvesting.

States have various rules regarding use of neem and its derivatives. Make sure to use only approved formulations.

NITRATE SALTS

Nitrate (NO_3) is the form of nitrogen most readily available to plants. Many nitrate salts, such as calcium nitrate ($Ca[NO_3]_2$) and potassium nitrate (KNO_3), provide a quick shot of soluble nitrogen for treating nitrogen deficiencies. Brands include Champion, SQM Hydroponica and Ultrasol.

NUTRIENTS

- CannaLot Medicinal, FedCo Seeds
- Geoflora Nutrients VEG and BLOOM, • Left Coast Wholesale
- Photosynthesis Plus, Microbe Life Hydroponics
- Nourish-L, Microbe Life Hydroponics
- Grow Booster , Reiziger
- Perfect Mix 3 part System, Sierra Naturals
- Royal Gold

OXYGEN

- O_2 Grow

Photo by Brian Valentine

PARASITOID WASPS

Several different species of wasp act as parasites on garden pests. These wasps are nonsocial, stingless to humans and so tiny that once you release them you may never see them again. The entire life cycle of parasitoid wasps revolves around the host pests. They lay their eggs in eggs, larvae or adult pests (depending on species), and the larval wasp then consumes the pest from within. Adult wasps often eat pests as well, depending on the species.

Choose the species depending on your pest:

- Encarsia species attack whiteflies. *Trichogramma* species go after caterpillars.
- Aphidius and Aphelinus species destroy aphids.
- *Dacnusa*, *Diglyphus* and *Opius* species for leaf miners.
- *Leptomastix*, *Anagyrus* and *Metaphycus* parasitize mealybugs and scale.

ENCARSIA FORMOSA WASPS (INDOORS AND OUTDOORS) FOR WHITEFLIES

The most successful biocontrol organism for the control of whiteflies in greenhouses is a tiny golden parasitic wasp called Encarsia formosa. Its preferred host is the greenhouse whitefly. A particular race, Nile Delta, attacks all major whitefly species so identifying the whitefly strain is not necessary. Adult wasps use sight and smell to find whiteflies. They lay eggs inside the whitefly larvae, preferably during their second instar. Whitefly larvae turn black as the wasp develops inside the body. After 15 to 25 days, the adult wasps emerge. It is most effective against the greenhouse whitefly and not as effective against the silverleaf or sweet potato whitefly. Three other parasitic wasp species, Encarsia luteola, Eretmocerus californicus, and Eretmocerus eremicus are commercially available for control of these species.

Buy them as pupae from companies such as Buglogical, Hydro-Gardens, IPM Labs, Natural Insect Control, Planet Natural and Rincon-Vitova. Plan on using about 100 pupae for every 100 square feet (9 square meters). Some pests may require multiple applications for full control.

PESTICIDES

- AzaGuard , Biosafe Systems
- BioCeres WP , Biosafe Systems

pH UP AND pH DOWN

pH-Up and pH-Down are generic terms for alkaline and acid pH adjustors, respectively. They are used to adjust water pH in indoor gardens and may come as either a powder or liquid. The active ingredient is usually potassium hydroxide (KOH) or potash (K2CO3) in pH-Up, or phosphoric acid (H3PO4) in pH-Down. Brands include General Hydroponics, GroWell, Growth Technology and many others.

Most fungi can grow only within a certain pH range. An alkaline solution with a pH of 8 makes the environment inhospitable for the fungus and stops its growth. Making up such a solution with pH-Down and applying it as a foliar spray is one of the simplest means of controlling foliar fungi such as gray mold and powdery mildew. It can be used on critically infected plants.

Many cannabis ailments are caused or exacerbated by improper pH and some pests are sensitive to the pH balance of a host as well, making regular monitoring and maintenance of your growing medium's pH a crucial control.

- TBN Naturals pH Up / Down
- pH Up and Down, Dakine 420

POTASSIUM BICARBONATE

Potassium bicarbonate ($KHCO_3$) is used in the food industry but is also useful as a fungicide against Fusarium, gray mold, powdery mildew and Septoria leaf spot. It is a wettable powder that raises the pH of the environment surrounding the fungi. Potassium bicarbonate is better than sodium bicarbonate (baking soda) because potassium is one of the macronutrients used by plants. It can be used to cure bad infections and weekly to prevent new ones. Potassium bicarbonate is also useful against potassium deficiencies.

Studies show that potassium bicarbonate is more effective as a fungicide when used with an oil and a wetting agent. Use 1 teaspoon (5 mL) of potassium bicarbonate, a teaspoon of oil and a small amount of wetting agent in a pint (500 mL) of water, or 3 tablespoons (45 mL) each potassium bicarbonate and oil and wetting agent as directed in a gallon (3.8 liters) of water. It is also available commercially in Ed Rosenthal's Zero Tolerance® fungicide, Armicarb100®, Kaligreen®, FirstStep®, Remedy®, Milstop® and other brands. Spray weekly as needed.

- Ed Rosenthal's Zero Tolerance Fungicide
- Subdue Maxx fungicide
- Green Cleaner, Central Coast Garden Products

POTASSIUM SALTS

Potassium sulfate (K2SO$_4$), potassium silicate (K2SiO$_3$) and potassium phosphate (K3PO4) are highly soluble salts that can be used to supplement a plant's potassium needs without introducing nitrogen (or phosphorous, in the case of the sulfate and silicate). Potassium sulfate is also sometimes called SOP (sulfate of potash). Brands include Champion, Pro-Tekt, Hydro-Gardens, Planet Natural and Allganic™ Potassium.

PREDATOR URINE

Deer avoid areas that smell of predators such as coyotes. Repellents based on predator urine exploit this behavior. Dog urine and even human urine can also be used, especially if the humans are meat eaters. Stale, strong urine is most effective.

Rather than applying these repellents directly to marijuana plants, create a barrier by applying them to other plants that grow around your garden. Another method is to string a rope or cord around the garden and tie cloth strips to the cord every 3 feet. Apply the repellent to the cloth strips to deter deer. Look for these repellents under brands such as CoyotePee® and Deer Busters® Coyote Urine.

- Predator Pee, Scent tags and urine

PREDATORY INSECTS

- Aphids, gnats, nematodes, mites, Natures Control

PREDATORY MITES

Set a mite to catch a mite. Predatory mites breed rapidly (especially indoors) and eat fungus gnats, spider mites and thrips. Look for species such as Ambly- seius, Galendromus, Hypoaspis, Neo- seiulus and Phytoseiulus.

Plan on using about 30 to 50 adults per plant, or 300 per 100 square feet (9 square meters). Note that while predator mites do reproduce quickly, they can't play catch-up with a rampant spider mite infestation. If your infestation is already out of control, then use a non-persistent insecticide to reduce the spider mite population before releasing predator mites.

Buy predatory mites as adults from companies such as Buglogical, Planet Natural, Hydro-Gardens, Natural Insect Control, Peaceful Valley and EcoSolutions.

- Galendormus Occidentalis, Biotactics
- Mesoseiulus Longipes, Biotactics
- Neoseiulus Californicus, Biotactics
- Neoseiulus Fallacis, Biotactics
- Phytoseiulus Persimilis, Biotactics
- Arbico

PREDATORY BENEFICIAL NEMATODES

These are microscopic creatures that live in soil and attack pests that spend their larval stages in soil, such as thrips and fungus gnats. Look for species such as *Steinernema* and *Heterorhabditis*. They can live for months in soil, so they can be applied as a preventive as well as to control existing infestations.

Unlike many beneficials, predatory nematodes are bought in bulk either as spray solutions or in sponges that you soak in water, then apply the water as a spray or soil drench. There are name brands such as NemaShield™ and Scan- mask. Buy from companies such as Buglogical, Planet Natural, Worm's Way, Hydro-Gardens, Natural Insect Control and Peaceful Valley. Coverage rates vary, so apply according to the manufacturer's directions.

- Entonem, Koppert
- NemAttackTM, Arbico

PSEUDOMONAS
This is a bacterial genus that contains several fungicidal species. Note that different Pseudomonas species are effective against different pathogens, so check the label to make sure that the one you're buying controls the diseases you're targeting. Pseudomonas products such as BioReleaf®, Blight-Ban® and Bac-Pack® control fungi such as gray mold, Fusarium and Pythium.

PUTRESCENT EGGS
In combination with garlic and capsaicin, rotten eggs are a potent deer repellent. Look for brands such as Deer-Off®. Apply as recommended by the manufacturer.

PYRETHRUM
Pyrethrum is a broad-spectrum natural insecticide, derived from a plant in the chrysanthemum family. It acts on contact and so must be sprayed directly on the target pests. It is effective against ants, aphids, caterpillars, fungus gnats, leaf miners, mealybugs, scale, spider mites, thrips and whiteflies. Note that pyrethrum is also toxic to many beneficial insects, fish and reptiles.

Pyrethrum is an organic insecticide, but some formulations include a synergistic additive, piperonyl butoxide, a powerful enzyme that interferes with insects' ability to filter out toxins.

Including it in the formula helps the pyrethrum stay in the insect's body longer but it is not considered safe for use with cannabis.

Pyrethrum is the natural extraction, but there are also synthetic versions called pyrethroids.

Pyrethroids use the same pathways, are effective, and low in toxicity. Mammals' metabolic processes quickly dismantle the pyrethroid's toxic effects, although high doses given to rats have produced some damage. Pyrethroids are synthetic compounds and are not considered organic and are not permitted in some areas.

Pyrethrum and pyrethroids do not persist in the environment and are quickly broken down by UV light and high temperatures so they do not cause any long-term contamination of soil or surfaces.

Use pyrethrum by spraying it directly on pests. Pyrethrum works by interfering with arthropod nervous systems, disrupting the neurotransmitters. They are paralyzed and die.

Pyrethrum kills ants quickly, so the ant foragers often don't have a chance to bring it back to the colony. This makes it less appropriate when the goal is to affect the total nest population.

Pyrethrum teas poured into colonies or mounds are fairly successful clearing out ants that are immediate problems. Use the pesticide as a drench to kill insect larvae in the soil. Follow manufacturer's instructions but use half strength two times a few days.

Pyrethrum formulations range from powders to sprays and are available under many different brand names, including Safer Yard and Garden Insect Spray, Planet Natural® Pyrethrum Powder and PyGanic Crop Protection.

Most states permit pyrethrum, but not with additives, many of which may be outlawed.

QUATERNARY AMINES

This is a class of compounds that act as broad-spectrum disinfectants. They are effective against many algae and many fungal pathogens, including gray mold, Fusarium and Pythium. Use these products for general disinfection of tools and hard surfaces, but do not use them directly on or around edible (or smokeable) plants. Physan 20® and Prontech® are popular quaternary amine preparations for horticultural use.

ROCK PHOSPHATE

Rock phosphate is a naturally occurring phosphate mineral. Used as a soil amendment, it releases phosphorous slowly and helps to prevent phosphorous deficiency. It is available in garden centers under brands such as Montana Natural, Peace of Mind and Espoma Organic Traditions.

Be careful to distinguish between rock phosphate and so-called superphosphate or triple phosphate. Rock phosphate is suitable for organic gardening, but the other two are prepared by treating rock phosphate with powerful acids to make a product that releases phosphorous much more quickly. Rock phosphate that has been processed in this way is no longer acceptable in organic gardens. It may release phosphorous too quickly for sustained vegetative growth.

ROSEMARY OIL

Rosemary will protect against insects

- SNS-209™

ROTENONE

Rotenone is one of the more toxic natural insecticides. It is a broad-spectrum insecticide that is also toxic to fish, small amphibians and even mammals, including humans. to a lesser degree. It acts by disrupting metabolism at the cellular level. Rotenone kills most chewing insects (including beneficials), but there are less-toxic alternatives.

Rotenone is banned from food crops, including cannabis, in some states, although it breaks down naturally in the environment over 7-10 days.

Rotenone is sometimes used as an adjuvant in combination with pyrethrum. Avoid products that contain rotenone Avoid products that contain rotenone.

- Liquid Rotenone Pyrethrin Spray, Bonide
- Biovision Rotenone, Careforde™ Safety & Scientific

SACCHAROPOLYSPORA SPINOSA
(BENEFICIAL BACTERIA) (Indoor and Outdoor)

This bacterium produces an insect toxin, spinosyns, which are a new class of organic insecticides, when it is cultured in a nutrient broth. They are effective against ants, caterpillars, leaf miners, spider mites, thrips, and other arthropods: In combination Spinosyn A and Spinosyn D., act by highly exciting the insects' nervous system to the point of dysfunction. Mortality is assessed at 100 percent. This combination acts when ingested and on contact. It does not affect non-target insects, such as beneficials. However, it is toxic to bees, so use outdoors with caution. It acts quickly; insects die within one to two days, but it must be eaten by them to be effective. It does not persist in the environment and breaks down into carbon, hydrogen, oxygen, and nitrogen when exposed to sunlight and microbes. It is marketed under the active ingredient name spinosad. Spinosad Brands include Monterey Garden Insect Spray, Captain Jack's Deadbug Brew, Conserve SC, and Entrust.

SESAME OIL

The oil pressed from sesame seeds has both insecticidal and fungicidal properties. It is effective against aphids, fungus gnats, gray mold, leaf miners, mealybugs, powdery mildew, scales, Septoria, spider mites, thrips and whiteflies. Sesame seed oil has both fungicidal and insecticidal properties. Sesame oil smothers
insects by clogging their spiracles, the breathing holes along their body, and
creates an unfavorable environment for fungi to take hold. You can also make
your own using sesame oil from a health food or gourmet shop. Mix it 1% (1
teaspoon per pint or 5 mL per 500mL) with water and a small amount of lecithin
and a wetting agent. It is available under brand names such as Organocide® (a
blend of sesame oil and fish oil) and Green Light® Bioganic® Home and Garden
(a mixture of sesame, clove, thyme, soybean and wintergreen oils).

SILICA AND SILICATE SALTS

Silica is not known to be essential for plant growth. However, when it is available
to them, plants absorb it through their roots. The plants park the silica in the cell
wall as well as internally in the cell. They also use it to form protective sheaths
near the leaf surface.

Farmers used to protect plants from fungal diseases using sprays made from
extracts of plants with high silica content such as the horsetail plant (Equisetum
arvense), which contains 15 to 40 percent natural silica. In controlled experi-
ments, plants with high silica content were protected against powdery mildew.
Silica is alkaline so one of its modes of action may be to create a no-grow environment for the fungus.

Plants grown with ample amounts of soluble silica grow thicker cell walls,
which results in stronger stems. It helps resist fungal and insect attacks. It also
positively affects the plants' sensitivity to absorption and translocation of several
macro- and micronutrients. It acts as a "toughening agent," increasing the plant's
ability to survive stressful situations such as drought, high salinity and nutrient
imbalance.

Hydroponically grown plants with soluble silicon added to the water solution
had reduced incidence and severity of powdery mildew in several trials. They also
had increased yields and produced thicker, whiter, healthier root systems. Foliar
silicon sprays also protect against powdery mildew.

Sources of silica include:

- Pyrophyllite clay is aluminum silicate in powder form. It can be applied as a dust or foliar spray and is available under a number of brand names (Seaclay, Mineral Magic, Pyroclay).
- Silica stone is a hydroponic medium used in place of clay pellets.
- Greensand is a popular soil and planting mix conditioner that can be used to supplement silica in soils.
- Vermiculite and perlite can be purchased in bulk at garden centers for use in potting soils. They are made from mica, which has a high silica content.
- EcoSand, Clino-Lite and ZeoPro are brands of zeolite mined from volcanic sites. They are composed of aluminum silicates, as well as calcium, iron, magnesium, potassium and traces of manganese and tin.
- Diatomaceous earth is made from the shells of tiny marine organisms that are very high in silica.
- Potassium silicate fertilizers re available commercially. Brands include Dyna-Gro Pro-Tekt®,

SILVER

Colloidal silver is a suspension of very fine silver particles. It has a long history as a general-purpose disinfectant, including use as an algaecide in pools and hydroponic systems. Used according to label directions, it will not harm marijuana plants. Several commercial brands are available, including Regal Pool Chemicals Silver Algaecide, Haviland Silver Algaecide and Silver Algaedyne®.

However, when sprayed on plants daily during early flowering it often causes hermaphroditism.

- Pro-TeKt® 0-0-3 The Silicon Solution®, DynaGrow
- Rhino Skin

SOAPS

Insecticidal soaps are mild soap solutions that damage the exoskeletons of soft-bodied insects (such as aphids, mealybugs, scales, spider mites, thrips and whiteflies) and cause them to dehydrate. They work by direct contact and so must be sprayed directly on the target pest.

You can make your own pesticidal soap solutions by mixing a few drops of a mild soap (the author prefers Dr. Bronner's Peppermint® castile soap) in a pint of water. However, some soaps can be toxic to plants, so always test a new soap by spraying it on a small area of one plant and waiting a day or two to check for damage. Commercial insecticidal soaps include Neudorff's Insecticidal Soap, Concern Insect Killing Soap, Monterey Quick, Safer Insecticidal Soap and M-Pede®. Soaps are also sold as algaecides under brands such as Schultz Garden Safe® Moss and Algae Killer and DeMoss®.

- Dr. Bronner's Soap

SODIUM BICARBONATE

Sodium bicarbonate ($NaHCO_3$), baking soda, has the same mode of action as potassium bicarbonate and is effective against the same diseases. It is often used by gardeners instead of potassium bicarbonate because it is readily available in most kitchens. However, it is not as effective as potassium bicarbonate and leaves sodium in the soil when it breaks down. Although I haven't heard of any cases where there was so much sodium buildup that it affected plant growth, it is prudent to use potassium bicarbonate.

For the purposes of cannabis cultivation it serves as a foliar treatment for powdery mildew that will change the pH of the leaf surface from roughly 7 to 8, making it inhospitably alkaline for most fungi including powdery mildew.

There is no problem with using baking soda at the first sight of powdery mildew. It works and has been used by finicky rose growers for more than 70 years. Use 1 teaspoon (5 mL) of potassium bicarbonate, a teaspoon of oil and a few drops of wetting agent or castile soap in a pint of water (500 mL), or 3 tablespoons (40 mL) each potassium bicarbonate and oil and a wetting agent or ½ teaspoon liquid castile soap in a gallon of water (3.8 L). Spray weekly.

- Ed Rosenthal's Zero Tolerance Fungicide
- Subdue Maxx fungicide
- Green Cleaner, Central Coast Garden Products

STREPTOMYCES GRISEOVIRIDIS (BENEFICIAL BACTERIA)

Streptomyces Griseoviridis is an actinomycete, a member of a curious group of organisms that fall in between fungi and bacteria based on gross morphology, but are truly bacteria. It colonizes the surfaces of plant roots. It produces metabolites that inhibit the growth of Fusarium, Botrytis, Rhizoctonia, and Pythium, and enhances the host plant's growth. S. griseoviridis prefers humid, soil, a wide range of soil pH levels, and temperature between 50°F and 68°F. It is also compatible with other growing additives, such as rooting hormones, and does not seem to affect other beneficial organisms. S. griseoviridis is available as spores and mycelial fragments in a powder. It grows a protective sheath around roots protecting them from attacks by pathogens. It also forms a bond with the roots that results in increased vigor and stress resistance. Use it to treat seeds, as a root dip, or soil drench. It is marketed as Mycostop.

STREPTOMYCES LYDICUS (INDOORS AND OUTDOORS)

For damping off, gray mold, powdery mildew, root rot, Verticillium wilt, and other pathogenic root fungi

Streptomyces lydicus is a naturally occurring common soil bacterium normally present in healthy "living" soil. When it is inoculated to improve poor soils and planting mixes, it provides protection against pathogenic fungi. It grows on the tips of plant roots, attacking pathogenic fungi. It can also be used as a foliar spray to treat powdery mildew and gray mold. S. lydicus grows well in normal garden temperatures and pH levels. The bacterium spreads along the plant's roots as they grow into the rhizosphere, which is the area around the root. This shields plant roots from pathogens. The bacterium releases an enzyme which weakens the fungus' cell wall as well as releases fungicides that inhibit the pathogen's growth. Use in early growth so it establishes early. S. lydicus does hinder mycorrhizal fungi growth. Hydrate the powdered bacteria by mixing it into soil mix. To use as a drench or foliar spray, mix it in water. It is safe for use around insects, other animals, and people. In hydroponic or sterile systems, introducing S. lydicus restores its natural presence on plants. In soil systems, adding Streptomyces lydicus elevates colony levels for increased benefit. It is available under the brand name Actinovate.

These bacteria produce fungicidal agents effective against gray mold, Fusarium, and Pythium. Brands such as MycoStop®, RootGuard® and Microgrow® contain Streptomyces formulations. These products are usually applied as a soil drench before symptoms appear.

SULFUR

Sulfur has been used to control gray mold, powdery mildew and Septoria for centuries. Several foliar sprays containing sulfur are available, such as Thiocal® and Safer® Defender Fungicide, but they may cause leaf damage. Check such products on a few branches and wait a day or two to check for problems before applying to your entire garden. The preferred delivery method for most marijuana growers is vaporization. Sulfur vaporizers use powdered elemental sulfur (also called garden sulfur), such as Thiolux Jet or Yellowstone Brand Hi-Purity Prill, heated in a container above a 60-watt lightbulb. The vapors condense into a fine film of very low pH sulfur granules on the leaf surfaces. The low pH environment inhibits fungal growth. Sulfur candles are available at some garden centers and work in a similar way.

Note that sulfur vaporizers produce a strong smell of sulfur. Air out your grow space after using a sulfur vaporizer. Sulfur should not be used with oils or when the temperature is over 85°F (29°C).

Check state regulations to make sure that use of sulfur is legal in your state.

In addition to its fungicidal properties, garden sulfur is useful for lowering the pH of alkaline soils and for correcting sulfur deficiencies.

• Sulfur Plant Fungicide, Bonide

TRICHODERMA (BENEFICIAL FUNGI)

Trichoderma is a genus of parasitic predatory fungi that develops a symbiotic relationship with roots. By wrapping itself around the roots it presents a physical barrier to pathogens. The fungi provide the roots with needed nutrients and use the root's exudates for nourishment. This increases plant resistance and vigor. The fungi also attack pathogens in the environment and use them for nourishment, too.

Several trichoderma species, such as *T. harzianum*, provide protection against fungal diseases including Fusarium, gray mold, Pythium, Septoria and Verticillium. PlantShield® and RootShield® use a particularly effective patented strain of *T. harzianum*: strain KRL-AG2, developed at Cornell University. Look for other brands also such as Trichodex®, Bio-Fungus® and BioTrek®. These products are applied as a soil drench for Fusarium, Pythium and Verticillium or as a foliar spray for gray mold and Septoria.

• Great White

UREA

Urea is not an organic fertilizer, but it is one of the best relatively available nitrogen sources. Because urea is so high in nitrogen (NPK 45-0-0), follow the label directions carefully to avoid nutrient burn. Brands include Espoma Quick Solutions Urea and many local and store brands.

- Lily Miller
- Jack's Fertilizer

UVC LIGHT

For bacteria, damping off, fungi, all molds, powdery mildew, and root rot. UVC light is considered deadly to life and kills the spores and tissues of powdery mildew, Pythium spp., Botrytis, and other fungal pathogens.

There are three ways that it is used.

First, there are water sterilizers that kill pathogens in the water supply. As the water passes around the UVC fixture, microorganisms receive fatal rays. The fixtures can also be used to clean inline water in recirculating hydroponic systems after filtration. Place the fixtures in the ventilation systems of growing rooms to kill fungi and bacteria spores before they enter the growing space. In closed areas use systems designed for sterilization in restaurants. The light is fatal to all airborne organisms passing through it. Some brands of lights are Big Blue, Turbo Twist, and Air Probe Sanitizer. Hand-held UVC wands and automated systems are used to prevent fungal infections. They kill powdery mildew spores on leaf surfaces. The light passes over each plant for only a second each day. This is enough to keep the plants fungus- free. Aeon UVC Systems is the only company manufacturing for the garden industry.

VINEGAR

Vinegar is toxic to powdery mildew. Use it at the rate of 1 tablespoon per quart (15 mL per liter) of water. Some gardeners recommend alternating vinegar with potassium bicarbonate and milk.

TRICHOGRAMMA WASPS (INDOORS AND OUTDOORS)

FOR CATERPILLARS

Wasps in the Trichogramma genus are also known as chalcid wasps. These small parasitic members\ of the order Hymenoptera are effective against many species of Lepidoptera. They lay their own eggs inside moth or butterfly eggs, which hatch into larvae that feed off the contents of caterpillar eggs. The eggs hatch

and go through growth and metamorphosis inside the Lepidoptera egg, emerging as adult wasps rather than caterpillars. They solve caterpillar problems without the introduction of any chemicals, natural or otherwise. As such, Trichogramma has become one of the most popular biocontrol measures by farmers and gardeners around the world. These wasps are so tiny, about 0.5 millimeter from one tip of the wing to the other, that you may not even see them. Adults have pear shaped wings with a single vein and fringed edges. The best use of Trichogramma is to release them when either moths or caterpillars are first sighted in the garden. Depending on the size and location, multiple weekly releases may be needed over a three to six week period. A good rule of thumb for each release is about one wasp per square foot.

Trichogramma are available commercially. Its pupae are glued to small paper or cardboard squares, which are placed in the garden. The wasps hatch and breed without any further effort on the part of the gardener.

WETTING AGENTS

This is a broad class of compounds that break the surface tension of water. This prevents water solutions from beading up on plant surfaces and helps them penetrate into soil. Castile soap (the author prefers Dr. Bronner's Peppermint®) can be used as a wetting agent. Commercial brands for organic gardening include Coco-Wet, ThermX™ 70®, Phyto Plus® Foliar Friend™, Natural Wet® and RainGrow Superflow™.

- Dr. Bronner's Soap

ZINC PHOSPHIDE

Zinc phosphide (Zn3P2) is an old rat poison now seeing a resurgence in popularity. It is fast-acting and more specific than some other poisons because it has a strong garlic odor that attracts rodents but repels most other animals. It is sold in baits under brands such as Nu-Kil®, Eraze™ Rodent Pellets, Prozap® Zinc Phosphide Oat Bait and ZP Rodent Bait AG. As with all rat poisons, zinc phosphide baits should be deployed in tamper-proof bait stations in accordance with the manufacturer's instructions.

ZINC SALTS

Zinc sulfate ($ZnSO_4$) and zinc oxide (ZnO) provide supplemental zinc in cases of zinc deficiency. Brands include Spectrum Chemical, BLU-MIN® Liquid Zinc Sulfate and NutraSul Plus 18% Zinc–Sulfur Fertilizer. It is also available in combination with Fe and Mn.

Sponsor Section

Thanks to all the businesses, organizations and individuals that supported this project.

Photo by Lizzy Fritz

Got Pests?

Biological Pest Control

Insecticides & Disease Control

Soil Health & Fertility

Monitoring & Trapping

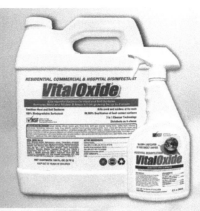

Simple All-in-One Products
For Commercial Growers

Trim Bin ™

High walls keep your work contained and make cleanup easy.

150 micron stainless screen produces only fine-grained, high-grade pollen.

Ergonomic design reduces back, shoulder and wrist fatigue.

Easily collect pollen with the static brush and mirror-finish collection tray.

Turn any chair into a comfortable workstation!

Increases productivity by alleviating user fatigue and discomfort.

Made in California.

HarvestMore ®

harvest-more.com

FIRST FOR
HYDROPONIC
CRAFTSMEN

REIZIGER.COM

Industrial Strength
HARVEST SOLUTIONS
Biomass, Cure, Store & Transport

100% BPA Free
FDA Approved
Contain Odors
Stabilize Moisture Level
Vacuum Sealable

Prevent Cross-Contamination
Save Time on Clean-Up
Maximize Shelf Life
Preserve Flavor and Freshness
Resistant to Punctures and Tears

Available in 10, 25, 100 PACK & BULK			
Volume	Name	Dimensions	Tips
Multi-Pack	Flock O' Bags	Varies	2 x Chicken Bags, 2 x Turkey Bags, 2 x Goose Bags & 10 x Quail Bags
3 Quarts	Quail Bag	8" x 16"	Holds ¼ lb, bag tied
2 Gallons	Chicken Bag	12" x 20"	Holds 1 lb, bag vacuum sealed
3 Gallons	Turkey Bag	18" x 20"	Holds 1 lb, bag tied
5 Gallons	Goose Bag	18" x 24"	Lines 5 Gallon Bucket
8 Gallons	8 Gallon Bag	24" x 40"	Holds 5 lbs, bag tied
27-37 Gallons	Bin Liner	48" x 30"	Lines 27-37 Gallon Tote Bins
20-30 Gallons	Ostrich Bag	30" x 48"	Fits 20 Gallon Trash Can or 30 Gallon Drum
55 Gallons	Drum Liner	36" x 48"	Based on Popular Demand Lines a 55 Gallon Drum
---	Bottomless Bags & Dispensers	12" x 100' 18" x 100' 24" x 100' 24" x 500'	Cut & seal to preferred size; Mountable Dispensers cut & store Bottomless Bags

True Liberty® Bags now offers True Liberty® Vacs
20" Gas-Purge, Vacuum and Impulse-Heat Sealer
Adjustable Settings and Industrial Strength Seal
Air Compressor powered Retractable Nozzle and Sealer Arm
Easy-clean glass vacuum filter system
Purge using gas of your choice
Rust-Treated, Powder-Coated Steel Chassis

GSD-15 & GSD-8
HIGH-EFFICIENCY CHILLED-WATER DEHUMIDIFIER

THERMAL
S O L U T I O N S

Commercial indoor growing business such as vegetable or cannabis growing needs significant dehumidification to avoid problems caused by moisture including mold, low productivity growth, and low quality or deteriorated biological plants. Typical air conditioners are not suitable for commercial dehumidification for indoor growing due to their high sensible heat ratio (SHR) with low dehumidification capacity and lack of capability in controlling temperature and humid independently, so only commercial dehumidifiers should be utilized.

GSD-15 & GSD-8

The GSD-15 and GSD-8 dehumidification units consume much less energy than traditional dehumidifiers for the same amount of water removal. Traditional commercial dehumidifiers work based on deep cooling to condensate moisture at low temperature and then reheating the cold air back to the temperature acceptable to the grow space. The deep cooling and reheat process consumes a lot of energy. GS Thermal Solutions' GSD units use a high-efficiency air-to-air plate heat exchanger to pre-cool the return air using the cold supply air off the primary cooling/dehumidification coil, essentially reducing the cooling load by 30 – 40% and eliminating the need to reheat. The use of chilled water from a chiller as cooling source makes the dehumidification units simple and reliable. In addition, the chiller with a water-side economizer provides "free" cooling without running compressors during winter when ambient temperature is low, even further reducing energy consumption.

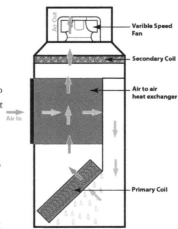

Patent Pending

Unit		GSD-15	GSD-8
Nominal Capacity*	(Tons*)	15	8
Performance	Water removal @80°F and 60% RH (lb/hr)	72	38
	Energy factor** (lb/kWh)	9.2	9.5
Fan	Nominal air flow (cfm)	3000	1600
	Nom. motor HP	4	2
Electrical		460-3-60, 277-1-60	460-3-60, 277-1-60
Control		VFD control for fan and water flow rate control based on actual load and setting	
Fluid	Fluid	Chilled water or propylene glycol	
	Entering temperature (°F)	42 ~ 45	42 ~ 45
	Flow rate (gpm)	up to 30	up to 16
Dimensions	inch	59"(W) 51.2" (D) 94.5" (H)	47.2"(W) 37.4"(D) 75.6"(H)
Piping Connections	Primary coil	1-5/8" OD	1-3/8" OD
	Secondary coil	1-3/8" OD	1-1/8" OD
	Condensate	1" ID	1" ID

NOTE

* Nominal capacity is based on that of traditional dehumidifier for the same water removal, and actual cooling requirement for this unit is much less

** Energy consumption Includes chiller power with EER 18 and fan power

GSD-15 & GSD-8 Features

- Most efficient commercial dehumidifier available on the market

- Automatic VFD fan speed control and water flow control according to load and temperature/humid setting

- Secondary coil to provide supplemental cooling or heating

- Quiet operation with high-efficiency, long-life fan

- HMI touch screen for parameter setting, monitoring, and control

- Can be integrated with central facility control through Modbus or BACnet

- Especially suitable for indoor growing applications with GS liquid-cooling LED lights

www.gsgrow.com

(203) 948-0542

ASK US ABOUT OUR PRODUCTS AND SERVICES

LIQUID COOLED LED

DEHUMIDIFICATION TECHNOLOGY

FACILITY CONTROL SYSTEM

ENGINEERING SERVICES

INDEX